LANCE

HOPE
IS ALIVE
ONE ADDICT'S STORY OF HOPE

Published by:

2410 W. Memorial Rd.
Suite C #260
Oklahoma City, OK 73134

nxtlevel.net

ISBN: 978-0-9882096-1-9
Printed in the United States of America
Library of Congress Cataloging-in-Publication Data

All scripture quotations, unless otherwise indicated are taken from The Holy Bible, English Standard Version® (ESV®) Copyright © 2001 by Crossway, a publishing ministry of Good News Publishers. All rights reserved. ESV Text Edition: 2007.

For information regarding author interviews or speaking engagements, please contact the public relations department – PR@lancelang.com.

CONTENTS

HOPE IS ALIVE:

ONE ADDICT'S STORY OF HOPE

by Lance Lang

For Ben & Annie

Thank you for sticking by me through the good times and the bad.

Though you are not always by my side, please know you are always in my heart.

May this book be an everlasting reminder that our God never stops loving us,

and that He is always pursuing us.

I love you both with everything I got.

Dad

FOREWORD

I got sober on July 16, 1985. I was 40 years old. I'd played in a Super Bowl and had been a member of the NFL's only undefeated team, the 1972 Miami Dolphins. But it wasn't long into my pro career before I started to live a life of defeat, losing over and over in the battle against alcohol.

Through an intervention from my family and several other friends that truly cared about me, I came to realize that my addiction was tearing up every facet of my life and that it was time for me to do something about it. I went into treatment and began a new life, a sober life.

During those first extremely painful and difficult nine months, the only thing I had to count on was *hope*.

I've since formed a relationship with Lance Lang, another man who has come to rely on hope. He has learned that honesty is the best tool you can have in recovery, tied closely to a strong faith in God. Lance is a man who is willing to share

7

both of them with just about anyone who'll listen.

Hopefully that's you.

In my own life, now looking at almost 30 years of sobriety, I *still* have hope that I can continue to live sober through doing and practicing the principles that Lance shares in this book, while walking this road of happiness and blessings. I hope you will find the peace and joy that Lance and I have found.

One of my favorite sayings I've ever heard came from my maternal grandfather. He would always say that he would rather see a sermon *walking* than to listen to one. In other words: show me, don't just tell me.

Well, Lance Lang is a walking sermon on hope. He is living proof that hope is alive.

I hope you'll listen to him. And then become one of those sermons yourself.

Jim Riley

Edmond, Oklahoma

February 2013

www.JimRileyOutreach.org

INTRODUCTION

Hope: a desire accompanied by expectation or belief in fulfillment.

"'For I know the plans I have for you,' declares the Lord, 'plans to prosper you and not to harm you, plans to give you hope and a future.'" –Jeremiah 29:11 (NIV)

For so many years I lived with no hope, no expectation my life would ever get better. My hope was dead, and along with it, any desire for a better life. For a decade I snorted or smoked everything I could get my hands on; an endless search for the rush of the first time propelled me to destroy and damage everything in my path. With fear as my empty motivator, I pointed the finger outward, blaming others for what my life had become. I was left feeling alone, stranded, different, and ultimately confused.

So I gave up.

"Screw it," I said. "Let's just do this."

So I did. Nothing else seemed to fix the problem, so I ramped up my pill intake to a near-lethal level and resigned myself to the idea that this desperate, reclusive state would be my life forever—at least until it killed me.

Thank God it didn't. In 2011, I experienced amazing grace and my hope was "shocked" back to reality. It was as if God swooped down, picked me up, and wrapped me in His finest robe. I had roamed this earth like a horse with blinders for so long, but God finally opened my eyes to a world I never knew existed, a world full of love and peace, overflowing with freedom and new friendships.

I've seen heroin addicts, meth cooks, coke heads, sex junkies, casino rats, blacked-out drunks, homeless freaks, and millionaire geeks.

I've seen them all. In some ways, I've been them all.

I grew up in a glass house, open seemingly for the whole world to see. Each disappointment and defeat pushed me farther and farther along my dark journey. As my obsession with getting high transitioned to addiction, I tried to stop. I would tell myself all kinds of things to try and trick myself into submission. Thoughts like these constantly tormented me:

Today I will do less.

Just try not to use until lunchtime.

You have to quit spending so much money.

You're gonna get caught.

Just take some tabs today, no oxys.

Okay, one more week and then... you have to quit.

The cycle that started when I was seventeen would ultimately end at 28. But along the way work pressure, divorce, poor choices, and unresolved pain took their toll. I was forced to take leave from a high-paying leadership position at a multimillion dollar company. I was humiliated in front of family members countless times and mortified as I stood in a courtroom, desperately pleading to see my children. I had absolutely no control, no hope, and no future outside of a daily purposeful pursuit to get high.

I look back at that time now and find it tough to even imagine how pathetic I was. The key is: as bad as my addiction was and as tragic as I looked to everyone around me, I couldn't see it. Sure, I knew I was hooked and would probably have admitted that pills and alcohol were ruining me physically.

But I couldn't separate myself from the addiction long enough to see what it was doing to my life, to my *entire existence.* I couldn't see the damage it was doing to my relationships, my kids, my job, my future.

It was devastating.

And I was hopeless.

A wise man once said that as long as matters are really hopeful, hope is mere flattery or platitude; it is only when everything is hopeless that hope begins to be strength. My hope became strength for me once I lost everything I valued. Looking back, the few times I experienced great success were not coupled with great hope, but mere expectedness. *This is what I deserve,* I would say to myself. *After all, I've worked hard.* It was not until my life had completely unraveled and all seemed lost that hope really became alive.

Hope surfaced, and has driven me to a freedom and satisfaction I had previously assumed were unattainable.

This book is the story of how my hope departed, how it was restored, and how I've kept it alive. I wrote it for drug addicts, alcoholics, gamblers, sex addicts, hurt people, prideful people, and angry people.

I wrote it for the fear-ridden, the guilty, the insecure, the obsessed, the perpetually disappointed, and anyone else caught in the tornado of destruction that is addiction.

The material is raw, personal, and to the point. This is not necessarily a guidebook to obtaining sobriety, although maybe someone reading this will be pushed to ask for help. More so, this book is geared to support addicts on their quest to maintain sobriety.

A Little About Me

Let's get one thing straight from the start: I am not a counselor. I am not a doctor. I am not a psychologist. Nor do I play any of those characters on TV. If you need guidance from a professional, then please go seek it out. (In fact, if you are reading this right now and know you need help with a chemical addiction, then please turn to the Appendix at the back of this book and call one of those recommended treatment centers. They're all full of devoted counselors, doctors, nurses, and staff members who would be more than happy to help you get started down your path to sobriety.)

So now that you know who I'm *not*, let's talk about who I *am:*

I am a drug addict.

A full-fledged, 100% addict.

But since I got sober, I've jumped into recovery with both feet. I've worked in one of the best treatment facilities in the country and have been mentored by one of the best interventionists and recovery advocates in the world. I've listened to countless lectures on drug and alcohol addiction, sat in over 700 small groups and meetings, and shared my story with innumerable groups, churches, and organizations.

But even more important than any training or educational experience, I wrote this book from my own experience. As you will read, God gave me the opportunity to accept this wonderful gift of sobriety, but it didn't come easily. I've had tons of help along the way, but if you've stayed sober for any amount of time, you know that no one on this earth can keep you from using except you. You have to earn your own sobriety, and you have to do it one day at a time.

Why did I write this book? Because it's my duty. By God's grace I've made it a few years and have some stories to tell, some advice to give, and some tips to pass along. That's what I have set out to do with this book: to provide an easy-to-read, modern guidebook not for *getting* sober but for *staying* sober in our current society.

The tips, tools, and principles you'll read don't just apply to those suffering from chemical addiction. For someone who picked up this book who hasn't shared my personal experience, don't just close it up now. Please read it, but whenever you see the words "drugs" or "alcohol," substitute your own cross to bear instead, whether it's gambling, sex, fear, depression, anger, guilt, loneliness… the list goes on.

It's been my experience that the majority of what you'll read will be applicable in a variety of areas in life. With that said, my focus is geared towards addicts and alcoholics, so keep that in mind.

A Little About the Book

Each chapter dives into a principle or growth area that is directly applicable to your life as a person in recovery. The chapters include personal stories and other tips and suggestions on how to implement these ideas, then close with a personal challenge designed to push you outside of your proverbial box—to give you a good stretch, if you will. I promise: though they might be uncomfortable or tough, if you follow the instructions and complete the challenge, you will grow. Do your best not to ignore these or just flip to the next chapter.

After the challenge, you'll see the header "Spiritual Application." What will follow is an applicable verse or collection of verses from the Bible, along with commentary relating to the previous chapter. If you're looking to further your connection with God, then read this section; if not, then move right along. Personally, renewing my relationship with God was the *single most important* aspect of my journey to stay sober. Without it, I would not be who I am today. No question.

Just as each person is created differently, so is every addict and that addict's recovery process. This isn't the first book on addiction; in fact it's the one millionth. I counted. This book is intended to complement your recovery process, not compete with it.

This book can enhance your aftercare plan, give you a jump start if you need one, or be a great tool for anyone coming off a relapse. Throw it into your daily readings for a few weeks or suggest it for a small group study with some other recovering friends. Better yet, take it your church or AA/NA group, or call up some friends and use it to start up your own program.

My Hope

My hope is that just one guy or gal will pick up this book and see a glimpse of themselves in my story. I pray they will find enough courage to raise their hand for help, to see enough hope in what God has done in my life since my intervention to believe that it's possible for them.

Maybe that person is you.

My hope is that a family member of an addict will pick this book up and begin to see addiction in a new light. That they will understand more of what's it's like on the "dark side" and thus be willing to lovingly come alongside their son or daughter, husband or wife, brother or sister, and support them in a more understanding and educated way.

Maybe *that* person is you.

Further, my hope is for today's generation, surrounded by a world that glorifies alcohol as the only way to have a good time, that abuses prescription drugs to escape reality at every turn, and in some states even legalizes recreational drug use. I hope this book can be the defibrillator paddles you need to shock your hope back to life.

Maybe *that* person is you.

No matter which person you are: buckle up, because

God has a huge plan for your life. It's full of freedom and joy. He is calling you to come away with Him, to join Him on a journey full of hope and love. His plan for you is still within your reach. It's going to be a wild trip—shoot, it may be your first *sober* trip! Regardless, the trip starts now.

Because hope is alive.

CHAPTER 1

MY STORY

"Commit to the LORD whatever you do, and he will establish

your plans."

--Proverbs 16:3 (NIV)

It was 10:15, the morning of April 6, 2011. I
was talking on my mobile phone in my office, staring
uncomprehendingly at my computer, eyes blurred, lethargic
and stoned. I'd just sniffed about 60mg of my typical morning
cocktail: 2/3 OxyContin, (enough to get me high for 30 minutes
or so) and 1/3 Lortab (to feel the burn). As I mentally withdrew
from the phone conversation, my head began to get heavy and I
started nodding off.

A few seconds later my head popped up violently to
pounding on my locked office door that could only come from
one person: my boss, who also happened to be my uncle.

"Lance!" he screamed. "Open the door!"

"Coming," I mumbled, hurriedly sliding all my drug paraphernalia into my top drawer and scurrying over to open the door. "Hey man," I said to my uncle as he stood in the doorway. "How are you this morning?"

"I'm fine," he replied sternly. "Come with me. We need to talk."

"O…kay," I answered slowly, following him.

We were halfway there when a rush of guilt hit me like Ray Lewis smashing into a tiny receiver coming over the middle. I knew I was in for it that day. It felt like I was walking to the principal's office; I just knew I was in trouble.

But let's pause right there, because to really grasp the rarity and severity of the conversation that was about to ensue, you need to understand my uncle and our relationship.

Uncle Pat

My Uncle Pat—my mother's brother—has three daughters and three sisters. I was the oldest grandson on that side of the family, and since there was a lack of boys running around, my uncle and I gravitated toward one another. I spent many holidays pestering him and, as most uncles do, he played some pretty good tricks on me as well. Countless times he conned me into believing he was going to take me duck-hunting in his neighborhood only to later realize how impossible (and illegal) that was, since he lived in the middle of the suburbs. Another time when I was 14, he convinced me that I could buy his old Jeep Cherokee for $1500 and drive it to school by parking a half-mile away and riding my bike the rest of the way.

Uncle Pat is a huge football fan, and while I was in high school, it was very common for him to drive two and a half hours from Oklahoma City to little old Pryor, Oklahoma just to watch me play on Friday nights. After those games, he and my dad would come up to my bedroom and we'd talk about the events of the game late into the night. He pushed me to stay in the weight room, eat more protein, practice harder... you know the drill.

Now, my Dad was always there for me and I will expound on him more later, but Uncle Pat was also a great mentor to me. So it was almost like a natural succession that I would eventually work for him when I got older.

I started working for Uncle Pat in the summer of 2005, on a four-month job in Seattle, learning the ropes of the telecommunications business, basic project management skills, and getting a general feel for working in a small-business environment. Needless to say, Seattle was quite a transition in culture and responsibility from my previous job working in the Wal-Mart corporate offices in small-town Arkansas.

As a side note, when I look back on that time in Seattle I am reminded of my abstinence from any mind-altering substances the entire time I was there. I was in a huge, brand-new city, 23 years old, living in a hotel—and I rarely even took a drink, much less smoked a joint or got gettered out. Interesting…

Anyway, I moved back to Edmond, Oklahoma later that year and began working at the corporate office of Uncle Pat's project management firm, CLS Group. Over the course of the next five years, he promoted me several times, and by the time I was 27, he had named me Vice President of the company.

Divorce

Just a little more background before we go back to that walk. Three months before I was named Vice President, I separated from my wife and watched as she and my two young children moved three hours away. That process—and the

22

subsequent dark period which followed—is when my addiction took hold. I became a complete wreck as I tried to manage the pain and guilt that covered my life. In an instant my wife, my children, and everything else that had kept me somewhat grounded since I was 18 were gone. Night after night I came home to a partially furnished house; rooms that had once been full were now completely empty, and I would literally cry myself to sleep. It was a devastatingly sad season of my life.

I had begun recreationally using pills (Lortab, OxyContin, Percocet) a few months before my separation. Mounting pressures were coming from all directions, so I did my best to party them away. Unfortunately this recreation wasn't anything new in my life—it had been there in some form since I was seventeen.

I always had something I was into—weed in the early stages, meth in the middle, and then the transition to opiates around my mid-twenties, with some coke and crack sprinkled in there along the way. As tough as it is to admit, I hardly had a time between the ages of seventeen and 28 where I wasn't cheating on life with some type of substance. Oftentimes, it was my main motivation for getting up in the morning—I'd dangle it over my head like a dog treat, rewarding myself whenever I could. Drugs were my second life, my alternate existence. I was one person to the world and another behind the scenes. The trauma of my divorce, the loneliness that ensued, and the discovery of the perfect drug (opiates) was the beginning of the end.

Teen Wolf

My first introduction to mind-altering substances came on a bright September afternoon in Pryor, Oklahoma. I was a junior in high school, sitting in the locker room after football practice, when a certain senior came up to me and said, "All right, Lance: ready to get high with me?"

This wasn't the first time he'd asked me that question. No, he'd badgered me for nearly *two months*, sometimes pointedly asking me in front of other team members, hoping to pressure me into it. Other times he asked in passing, like a nonchalant request along the lines of, "You want fries with that?"

Something was going on with that guy, and though I didn't know what it was for sure back then, I now think he was really just reaching out for someone to hang out with, someone to join him in his misery.

24

Nevertheless, with each proposal, I inched closer and closer to saying "yes." My imagination would spin out of control wondering what it would be like, what might happen, or how fun it possibly could be.

I never considered what it may lead to.

So when this teammate casually asked me the same question that fateful day I'd heard so many times before, I finally responded, "Yeah, let's do it."

He was stunned and surprisingly happy all at the same time. We quickly finished changing clothes and took off to his house, where my education into all that is smoking pot began. He showed me the ropes, pulled out his little red pipe, grabbed his dirty bag of shake, loaded the bowl, and we were off.

The next thing I really remember was driving around my little hometown in their Ford Bronco with this guy and his older brother, blaring the Metallica song "Master of Puppets" while they recited every word.

Master!

Master!

Over and over and over and over again it resounded. I was officially freaked out. Seriously, I was stunned. *Who are these people?* I thought. Furthermore: *What is this song and why have I never heard it?*

MASTER!

MASTER!

My head spun and my heart raced a thousand miles an hour. But as crazy and weird as it all was, I remember also feeling like I had just found a new club, like I was instantly initiated in to a new fraternity that spoke its own language and connected on a wavelength normal people had no ability to reach. I had never seen anyone act the way there were acting. I wasn't sure exactly what was going on or how I felt about it, but I knew one thing for sure:

I wanted more.

Their dad was home when we got back to their house, and that began my first of a thousand sessions with paranoia. I quickly realized I wanted no part of talking to that dude. I mean *zero*. First of all, he barely knew me, so he started in with all the typical "get to know ya" questions, and by round two, I found myself about to vomit on his couch. Secondly, he was huge. A big, scary, gruff-looking guy. So I waited for a break in the conversation, then not-so-subtly dashed out the front door.

History was made; my first dance with Mary Jane was in the books.

Childhood

When I sit down and analyze it, though, I realize my battle with addiction started at an extremely early age, well before that locker-room incident, when I became fascinated with collecting the most random of things and doing it to gross excess. I hoarded everything my obsessive-compulsive little mind could think of: sports cards, turtle figurines, knives, used toothbrushes, matchbooks, aluminum foil (I had the biggest ball of aluminum earth has ever seen—seriously it was huge... Volkswagen-huge), catalogs of all sorts (remember when you could call an 800 number from a TV commercial and they would send you a catalog of certain products? Think Soloflex or Bowflex). You know: the stuff everyone collects, right?

The point is not the wide variety of junk I collected, but the fervor and drive I had while doing it. I fixated on the idea that I could collect the most of an item and then, for some insane reason, might receive a prize from others based on my huge collection of Soloflex catalogs.

You see a major part of my addictive personality is also people-pleasing.

As I grew, my obsessive behavior transitioned from collectible items and kitchen supplies into athletics. When

I got into a sport, I *really* got into it, playing day and night. Basketball was really my first love and is still my favorite game to play. I pushed my dad to shoot hoops with me, or made my sister set invisible screens so I could work on my pick-and-roll technique. Anything I could do to get out there and play more, I would do it.

My obsession didn't manifest itself in the actual exercise or playing of the games, but rather in the competitive nature of the sport. For example, when I was in third grade, I often ran home from school, grabbed my ball, and headed to the driveway for free throw practice sessions. I would line up and go through my routine: four dribbles, a breath, and then shoot. I would repeat that pattern for *hours*.

That's normal, right?

But it gets better. Because after every ten shots, I ran into the garage and logged my results in a little spiral notebook, appropriately entitled "Basketball." (I think I still have that notebook somewhere). There I was in *third grade*, obsessively logging my driveway free-throw percentages. I mean, we are talking about *practice*.

I had other notebooks as well. When I got into baseball, I had a logbook for every stat for the entire season. I kept it in the dugout and recorded the statistics in between innings. My obsession with stats and numbers grew into selfish preoccupation as I began to force my mother to keep an official stat book for all my basketball games in the fifth and sixth grades. I assure you there were no other eleven-year-olds at the Kenwood Elementary Invitational Tournament running up into the stands between games asking their mommies about their first-half field goal percentage.

When my mom couldn't make one of our games, I asked my friend's mother to "keep the book" for me, and she gave me the most perplexed and stunned looked I had ever seen. Now, she did it and did a fine job (although I still think I had six assists that game, not five), but it's funny how we hold on to certain moments from our childhood and never let them go. That moment—the memory I have of that poor woman's stunned face—served as an epiphany for me as I worked through the recovery process later, revealing how and why I have such an addictive personality.

The process of growing up, however, was more than just crazy collections and obsessive behaviors. A large part of why I am who I am relates to the environment in which I was raised. I am a "PK," or "pastor's kid." My Dad was the pastor of First Baptist Church in Pryor, Oklahoma, a church that regularly ran between 800-1000 people each Sunday, in a town of roughly 8000.

Needless to say, most everyone knew who I was, so I felt the eyes everywhere I went, and unfortunately my parents received many phone calls. It was hard to grow up that way, and there's no excuse for my behavior, but it's certainly part of my story.

I compared it earlier to living in a glass house. I was down here, running around and being a kid, sometimes getting into a little trouble but usually having fun... okay, getting into *a lot* of trouble... but then there were those above me, looking down and shaking their fingers with disapproval. I saw them as a group of judgmental haters waiting to catch me, waiting to pick up the phone and say, "Pastor, do you know what your *son* just did?"

Live like that for very long and after a while you just say, "Forget it. I can't please anybody, so I'll just go do whatever I want to do, whenever I want to do it."

Walk of Shame

Back to that April day in 2011... Uncle Pat and I

stepped into his office and I took a seat in front of his big, bold, dark brown desk. In that moment, I knew what was about to happen. I knew he was going to ask me what was wrong. I knew he hoped to get some details out of me.

But I wasn't going to tell him. I had too much to lose.

For years I had worked with everything I had to protect my secret (only later would I find out what a horrible job I had done covering up what had been glaringly obvious). Nevertheless, on that day, as guilty as I was, I wasn't about to admit it. I had spent that long walk working up a mental defense, so I was ready to argue as soon as he opened his mouth. We spent the first 15 minutes or so disputing work stuff: collection issues, personnel problems, projections, etc. After several rounds of arguing, voices rising and fists pounding on the desk, both our emotions had skyrocketed, and that's when it happened.

Uncle Pat stared me down from across that big, mahogany desk and peered into my soul like no man ever had before. "Lance," he said, "what is *wrong* with you?"

My head instantly dropped. I had used up all my emotional resources during our argument, and the high-pressure, serious conversation had made my chemical high wear off like some cheap Tim McGraw cologne. I had no energy left.

As sweat beaded on my forehead, he continued: "For the past year you have been late to work every day. You're lazy, lethargic. You yell and scream at your employees. You're territorial and temperamental. Half the time I can't find you or get hold of you, and when I do, you lie about where you are and what you're doing. I'm sick of it, and you are *not* leaving my office until you tell me what's going on and we figure out what we're going to do about it."

When he finished, I knew I was finished.

I hung my head, weighed down by all the guilt and pain of the divorce, the professional disappointment I had become, and the destruction of every relationship I cherished, and tears began forming in my eyes. Drug use had shut my body off from any true emotion whatsoever, so they started slowly, one by one, trickling down my face.

But as I mustered the energy to raise my head and look at the man confronting me, with the reality looming of what I had become, I began to weep. Uncontrollably. I cried for what seemed like hours as I began for the first time ever to paint the mental picture of what my life *really was like*. Why I looked

32

the way I did, where I would go when I would disappear, what drugs I was taking, and how I couldn't stop no matter how hard I tried.

That day I finally got honest. I told Uncle Pat about the pain and darkness that overtook me in my reclusive state. I related how I felt I was losing my mind. How I was seeing things, hearing voices, and doing things I never thought I would do.

For a long time I couldn't explain why *that* was the day I chose to let it all out. It wasn't like I hadn't been confronted, accused, or even caught before then. I had. Several times. On a couple occasions, I was caught red-handed stealing from family members and yet I still wouldn't admit it.

So why was this the day? Why this random April morning? Was it the tone my uncle used when he confronted me? Was it the fact that I was just emotionally and physically drained because of I was running out of pills?

No, it wasn't any of that stuff.

It's simple, really: I was tired of fighting.

Addicts reading this book will understand that there comes a time when you just can't fight anymore. Time catches up with you and you simply can no longer wage war against the pain, the withdrawal, the dealers, the money, the lies, the guilt, the shame. A time comes when you can't endure the endless disappointing looks from your children, or the heartache you cause to those you love most.

You just get to a point where you hit rock-bottom and you see no other way out.

That's what happened to me that day.

I was done. I was finished fighting.

I was defeated.

And *I knew it.*

So began my journey down the road to recovery, my life completely altered from that moment forward. Like a rock in a slingshot, I was instantly propelled toward forgiveness and restoration. It's been a long road; a road that has alternated between excruciating discomfort and overwhelming gratitude.

My addiction was more than just snorting dozens of OxyContin and pounding Red Bull vodkas all day. Those antics and behaviors were just symptoms of a far deeper problem ingrained within my obsessive soul—my personality and temperament are bent in that direction. I've always searched for what would make life better, what would take me *higher.* Call this internal drive whatever you want: a disease, a personality trait, a behavior... I don't really care.

I call it a problem.

It's a problem that, if I don't treat it *every day*, will destroy my life. If I fail to surrender, if I ignore my powerless state, I will slide back to that dark place where I was driven to the depths of insanity; a dark hole I barely made out of alive. Anthony Keidis, the lead singer of the Red Hot Chili Peppers said this of that dark place:

> *When you're using drugs, you're driven by this mystical black energy, a force inside you that just won't quit. And the weaker you get, the more you feed into that energy, and the more it messes with you. When your spirit becomes dark and your lifestyle becomes dark, your existence is susceptible to infiltration by dark spirits. I've seen it so many times with addicts. You can see that they're controlled by dark energy, the way they look, their appearance, their voice, their behavior, it's not them.* [FOOTNOTE: *Scar Tissue*, by Anthony Keidis with Larry Sloman, Hyperion Books, 2004, p. 335]

There is no easy or soft way for me to explain my

plight. I wish there was, but there just isn't. It is in this harsh reality, however, where my new life begins. Coming to grips with who I was, and realizing what I had to do allowed my hope to start breathing again, awakening and filling my lungs with fresh air.

Spiritual Application

Jesus continued: "There was a man who had two sons. The younger one said to his father, 'Father, give me my share of the estate.' So he divided his property between them.

"Not long after that, the younger son got together all he had, set off for a distant country and there squandered his wealth in wild living. After he had spent everything, there was a severe famine in that whole country, and he began to be in need. So he went and hired himself out to a citizen of that country, who sent him to his fields to feed pigs. He longed to fill his stomach with the pods that the pigs were eating, but no one gave him anything.

"When he came to his senses, he said, 'How many of my father's hired servants have food to spare, and here I am starving to death! I will set out and go back to my father and say to him: Father, I have sinned against heaven and against

you. I am no longer worthy to be called your son; make me like one of your hired servants.' So he got up and went to his father.

"But while he was still a long way off, his father saw him and was filled with compassion for him; he ran to his son, threw his arms around him and kissed him.

"The son said to him, 'Father, I have sinned against heaven and against you. I am no longer worthy to be called your son.'

"But the father said to his servants, 'Quick! Bring the best robe and put it on him. Put a ring on his finger and sandals on his feet. Bring the fattened calf and kill it. Let's have a feast and celebrate. For this son of mine was dead and is alive again; he was lost and is found.' So they began to celebrate.

"Meanwhile, the older son was in the field. When he came near the house, he heard music and dancing. So he called one of the servants and asked him what was going on. 'Your brother has come,' he replied, 'and your father has killed the fattened calf because he has him back safe and sound.'

"The older brother became angry and refused to go in. So his father went out and pleaded with him. But he answered his father, 'Look! All these years I've been slaving for you and never disobeyed your orders. Yet you never gave me even a

young goat so I could celebrate with my friends. But when this
son of yours who has squandered your property with prostitutes
comes home, you kill the fattened calf for him!'

"'My son,' the father said, 'you are always with me,
and everything I have is yours. But we had to celebrate and
be glad, because this brother of yours was dead and is alive
again; he was lost and is found.'"

—Luke 15:11-32 (NIV)

The parable of the prodigal son really says it all for me. It's my story, and I know many of you feel the same way. I am so thankful that God in His mercy brought me home to Himself. Perhaps you find yourself in a faraway place, far removed from the Heavenly Father. As you seek God through the Bible and the Big Book, it is my prayer that, in your desperation, you will be reminded that your Heavenly Father desires to welcome you home.

The story of the prodigal son starkly reveals that the prodigal had to remove himself from his "pig pen" and go to his father's house. Until you get to the place that your desire to be "home" is greater than your desire to live in the "wallow of this world," your life will remain in the sick, twisted, disgusting, famine-ridden world of self. But God will *always* welcome you home with great fanfare! Living clean and sober is right there, waiting for you, and *hope is alive*!

CHAPTER 2

SURRENDER

"Do not be conformed to this world, but be transformed by the
renewal of your mind, that by testing you may discern what
is the will of God, what is good and acceptable and perfect."
--Romans 12:2 (ESV)

"I have been driven many times upon my knees by the
overwhelming conviction that I had no where else to go"
--Abraham Lincoln

Uncle Pat and I sat in a conference room a few
days after that intervention, huddling around a telephone
and listening intently to Jim Riley, one of the foremost
interventionists in the country, as he explained what the next
few days of my life would look like. He laid out the details
of the detox facility I would enter, and listed the rules and
40

regulations I would have to follow.

The more he talked, the more it became glaringly obvious that agreeing to sobriety would force me to give up any real sense of control over my life as I knew it. As my mind began to play out this uncomfortable scenario, the reality of my situation became tragically clear. Jim went on to finish the general itinerary for the next few weeks and then suddenly came to an abrupt pause. He cleared his throat as if to elevate the mood to a higher level and asked me this question: "Son, what are you willing to do?"

I sat back in my chair, reflecting on all the "right" answers as they stumbled through my mind:

Anything.

Whatever it takes.

Whatever you say.

Verbalizing those answers, however, scared me to death. Why? Because even at that point I was *still* using. In fact, I was fairly high *at that moment*, so committing to doing "whatever it took" or "anything they asked" went against everything my mind and body were telling me to do.

I'd been doing whatever I wanted to do whenever I wanted to do it for so long I wasn't sure it was possible to stop.

41

I had been running all over the state chasing my next fix, and leaving a tornado of destruction and heartbreak along the way. I'd built the walls around me so tall most people had quit trying to climb over them to help me. With each passing day, those walls got taller and taller and taller, leaving me in a destitute and isolated place.

So the fear of turning my life over to anyone else was terrifying, almost crippling. But even in the midst of the fog in which I lived, I knew the importance of my response to the question Jim was posing. For some reason on that day, God gave me a moment of clarity. Everything in my mind and body lined up and I knew my answer.

I leaned forward, hung my head over the telephone, and said, "Sir, I'm willing to surrender. To do whatever it takes."

I had no idea where that response would soon lead me.

I look back and although I still had miles and miles of hurdles to clear, I picture that moment as the first positive choice I made towards changing my life.

After a brief stay at The Referral Center in Oklahoma City, I soon entered a treatment center named Rob's Ranch and had one of my first counseling sessions with Mr. Bruce Kaup. I'd heard quite a bit about Bruce before that day, and all that he'd accomplished throughout his amazing 30-year career as a drug and alcohol counselor.

"He's the best in the country," I was told.

"He's a mind-reader," one of the other patients told me as I was checking in.

"He's gonna make you cry like a baby," another one warned.

That last comment almost made me turn around, check back out of the treatment center, and go get high. I mean seriously, what grown man wants to be told that another man is going to make you *cry*? Not this guy. But I digress. Although everything said about Bruce turned out to be true, especially that part about making me cry, his approach to me that first day was totally unexpected and completely took me off guard.

It was a warm April day, so we took off on a walk around the facility and not more than twenty steps into it, Bruce turned to me and said, "Lance, do you know what being powerless means?"

After rolling the word around in my head and failing to come up with a suitable answer, I responded with a simple and honest, "No, I guess I don't."

Over the next thirty minutes, we walked around and

around that facility, Bruce slowly and patiently describing to me the principle of powerlessness and the ways it related to my addiction. He told me over and over again that I had no power to change the fact that I was an addict. He continued to remind me that I was chemically dependent, and regardless of how the addiction or dependency got me, I was an addict, and that's that.

I listened and deliberated and began to mount a defense. Thinking that he was talking down to me or accusing me of something, I honestly got a little upset. However, before I could muster up a string of words to respond to his diagnosis, Bruce stopped walking, looked me in the eye, and finished what he had to say. "Lance," he said, "I am not trying to talk down to you. In fact, everything that I said to you, I must say to myself daily as well."

Bruce went on to explain that, when defended with our own power and might, this plague of addiction will defeat us every day. "You can't out-work addiction," he said.

That really hit home to this workaholic.

He went on to finish: "Lance, what you need to begin thinking about, at least for the first few weeks, is that this addiction has you beat. It's defeated you. So instead of continuing to fight it for years and years and watching it destroy what's left of your life, why not just consider surrendering to it? Accept it as it is. Claim that it got the best of you and admit you are powerless over it."

Boom! That hit me like Marquez smashing Pacquiao with that right hook! Bam! Immediately it made sense and sudden relief rushed through my veins, breathing life into my body. As I mentioned earlier, I was so tired of fighting at this point in my life that surrendering sounded like a much-needed vacation.

Surrender came naturally to me. It was logical. As Bruce described the process, it became so clear how, over a period of time, I slowly lost any power over my drug and alcohol use. I had begun to do things that I'd promised myself I would never do at all.

I compared it to the familiar analogy of the frog and the boiling pot of water. I'm sure you've heard it before: put a frog in a pot of water on a stove top and slowly turn up the temperature, the frog will just sit there without realizing that the water he is sitting in is increasing to a scolding hot level. The next thing little Kermit knows, he's dead. Done. Over. He just sits there while his mind and body trick him, telling him,

"You're okay; you've been here before; this water ain't got nothin' on you."

But what he should be doing is freaking out, jumping around, and screaming at the top of his froggy lungs, "This is *hot*! This is *hot*! Get me out!" Unfortunately because of this little amphibian's abnormal mental and physical adjustment, he instead accepts the insanity and craziness as being normal. Typical. *Status quo.* This incrementally warming pot of water is no different than a pond or lake.

That is what my life had become. A series of crazy situations compounded by heart-breaking loneliness and depression, a day-in/day-out continuous cycle of insane behavior that had become normal existence to me. Skipping work to meet my dealer 90 minutes away in Tulsa, driving back home, inhaling $70 worth of sushi, and throwing up all night was my typical Wednesday. Bouncing checks, pawning stolen jewelry, stealing pills from my poor grandparents—all were common activities I did with no remorse.

In that moment with Bruce, as I looked back on my life, I could finally *see* the insanity. Accepting that it was out of control then became an easy choice. Having even a few days of sobriety under my belt gave me a perspective I had not had before.

As we continued to talk, Bruce listed some aspects of my life and asked me, as a result of my newfound understanding of powerlessness, if I had any real control over any of them. Read through his list and ask yourself the same question: Do you have any true control over or are you powerless concerning...

- Drugs and alcohol
- Your family
- Your spouse
- Your boss
- Your coworkers
- The weather
- God

Of course my answer was no. I didn't have power over any of these areas. This may sound simplistic to you, but realizing this concept completely and utterly flipped my world around. I was so obsessive-compulsive; I had to always be in control, I had to be the one pushing other people around, directing the flow, manipulating the situation. That was tiring work, and when I failed or something didn't go the way I wanted, I had no positive way to cope with it. I had no release except to snort line after line of OxyContin until the world was so far away I could barely see it.

This manifested in every situation I encountered, whether it was losing a big client at work or a rainy day that ruined a golf outing. I couldn't properly deal with either one, so I searched for a medicating solution. The outcome was always the same: I got high. Escaped reality and found myself in the apathetic state.

Admitting vs. Accepting

It's one thing to understand the concept of powerlessness; it's entirely different to surrender to it daily.

You may have heard thousands of times that admitting you have a problem is the first step. Well I couldn't disagree more. Admitting the problem was nothing. You can admit to anything, especially when being pressured or confronted with the dreaded "choice" question. I can't tell you how many stories of recovery I have heard that have started with this line: "Well, I was given a choice…" Typically that's followed by "…to go live on the streets, homeless with no support or to 'admit' I had a problem and agree to check into treatment."

While lives *can* be changed in this situation, the

admission of the inherent problem is *not* a step in the actual "recovery" process—it's just a public acknowledgement of what the rest of the world has witnessed for years.

The first step, the most important step, and yes, the most difficult step for most people, is initial acceptance of the problem and continual acceptance *every day* from that point forward. The difference may sound subtle to you, but it's not.

Think about it. Admitting you have a problem can easily be lip service, done to appease family, the justice system, a boss, or a spouse who's had enough. But true daily acceptance of your addiction requires you to get up each morning and choose to surrender. As one of my other counselors would say: choose to live in the solution, not the problem.

"Why is this so important?" you may be thinking. "I thought this book was geared to folks who already had some sobriety under their belt. If I'm sober, I've already surrendered. That's why I am here."

Well, you may be right. Maybe you *have* surrendered and are doing just fine. But many of us—even after experiencing time in a treatment center or working through the steps with a great sponsor—have a mind with a strong propensity to work against us. It fills us with scary thoughts like these:

- *I made it. I stayed clean longer than I ever thought I would.*
- *What's a couple of beers gonna hurt?*
- *I can hang out with those people; I'm strong enough now.*
- *No more drug tests, I'm in the clear now.*
- *I got a job and my legal issues are over; why not see if I'm really addicted?*
- *Alright, the wife trusts me again. Let's have some fun.*
- *I can smoke a little weed. It's not gonna hurt me.*
- *I was never really an alcoholic anyway.*

Some of you have already had these thoughts—and many more just like them. That is why a choice to surrender must be your first step every day. Each morning should start out with a purposeful action to live in the solution, not the problem. A mental, emotional, and yes, even a physical surrender to your addiction.

By doing this each morning, you set the tone for how you will address the problems, questions, issues, successes, temptations, and triggers you will face the rest of your day.

This act of surrender reminds me of my buddy Floyd Carter. Floyd's a big fisherman and loves nothing more than to greet a beautiful fall morning by jumping in a john-boat and hitting the open water. Choosing to surrender each morning is similar to ol' Floyd choosing to place his hand on that throttle and steer his way across the water. He must at all times avoid danger and other boats. His body is always facing forward, toward the front of the boat. He constantly looks ahead so he can see what's coming at him. The whole body of water is in his purview.

Apply this analogy to your life. When you choose to surrender daily, you automatically position yourself in a forward-facing posture. Your vision is clear, your state of mind balanced. You can clearly see danger ahead of you as it presents itself. You see your old friends or old triggers, you know what will happen if you get involved and you steer away from them. You choose to circumvent the hazardous situation. By surrendering daily, your eyes are wide open to who you are and what you must avoid to stay clean and sober. When trouble arises, you simply steer the boat in another direction.

The opposite holds true as well. By getting up each

morning and choosing not to surrender or even failing to acknowledge who you are, you become like a man in that same john-boat who refuses to put his hand on the throttle. He sits there in his seat and sees the whole world coming at him and throws caution to the wind. He just lets the boat go wherever it wants. He flies around the lake with no direction, no guide.

What happens to that guy? Well the boat either loses control and crashes or it drifts over to areas where he doesn't want to go fish. Either way, it's not good. Either way he doesn't get the result he is looking for.

So what results are you looking for? What type of life are you choosing to live? Are you willing to surrender? Are you willing to do whatever it takes or do you still want to fight?

I urge you to choose the latter. Choose to surrender daily.

CHALLENGE

Acceptance and surrender are principles that must be applied and put into action *daily*. As you complete this challenge, the course of daily surrender will become a part of who you are, a frame of mind, a state of your soul to guide you through years of living clean and sober.

1.   Head over to your local art supply or craft store.

2.   Ask for a small, white flag.*

3.   Buy the flag and take it home.

At home, take some time to reflect on what you've learned in this chapter. Consider everything it might require you to do, to give up on, or to walk away from.

Are you ready to surrender your life to sobriety?

If your answer is yes, then with a bold, dark Sharpie, write these words on your flag:

"I surrender."

Next, place your flag over your door. In a similar fashion to the way football teams slap the "play like champions today" sign or touch the school's sacred rock as they leave the locker room to take the field, allow this sign to be a daily reminder for you. Each time you leave your room, look at it. Reach up and touch it as you leave, even if you have to jump up and slap it. Do it! Make this a commitment.

By choosing to do this you are saying, *I am choosing to live in the solution. I resolve to say no to my old way of doing things, my old way of thinking, my old way of acting. I know where that leads me and I don't want to go there anymore.* This is an act of daily surrender!

* If you can't find a flag, then a piece of paper will work. But remember, the more you put into this, the more you will get out of it!

Spiritual Application

"Humble yourselves, therefore, under the mighty hand of God so that at the proper time he may exalt you, casting all your anxieties on him, because he cares for you. Be sober-minded; be watchful. Your adversary the devil prowls around like a roaring lion, seeking someone to devour. Resist him, firm in your faith, knowing that the same kinds of suffering are being experienced by your brotherhood throughout the world. And after you have suffered a little while, the God of all grace, who has called you to his eternal glory in Christ, will himself restore, confirm, strengthen, and establish you."
—1 Peter 5:6-10 (ESV)

This passage is such a great reminder of what God did for me and sums up what God can do for you.

My first step in surrender was to humble myself. After years of trying to do things "my way," it became clear I had encountered a foe I was helpless to overcome. I had to accept

54

defeat. I quickly realized: not only did I need to surrender myself to my addiction, but I needed to surrender my *entire life* to my Savior. With God on my side, I could freely give Him my cares and anxieties, releasing my soul from the worries and heaviness I had been carrying around for years.

Furthermore, we see in this passage that God commands us to be sober-minded and on alert. He warns us that there is an adversary who's out for our blood, plotting a course to steal and even kill.

But God doesn't leave us to fight our enemy empty-handed. No! He brings alongside us a "brotherhood," a team of people from all over the world who know our experiences and have suffered as we have.

As we follow this first action, humbly surrendering our hearts to God, He promises that He will eventually restore, confirm, strengthen, and establish us in His time, setting us on a course for a new life free from the toils of addiction.

CHAPTER 3

"HOPE" PARTNERS

"When your teammate looks you in the eye and holds you

accountable, that's the greatest kind of leadership there is."

--Doug Collins, Philadelphia 76ers Coach

"The mind is not a vessel to be filled, but a fire to be kindled."

--Plutarch

"Though one may be overpowered, two can defend themselves.

A cord of three strands is not quickly broken."

--Ecclesiastes 4:12 (NIV)

Most addicts face a pretty steep, uphill climb as we try
to transition back into mainstream society. We fight labels and
stereotypes. Our past decisions seemingly lurk around each
corner, waiting for the worst possible time to jump up and snag

us. If we had insecurities *before* we found sobriety, they're even more prevalent as we step back into a world where we constantly feel the proverbial finger being pointed at us. We see the snickers and hear the gossip.

Furthermore, when we walk into establishments or organizations we once frequented, we can feel the heaviness our presence carries. Oftentimes people are downright scared of us, tiptoeing around us, as if one false move will send us off into the bathroom with a needle or drink in hand.

I know this feeling very well. I've been there, just like many of you have. The first day I came back to work after getting sober, I felt all my coworkers' eyes following every step I took. My Uncle Pat had graciously kept my job open for me while I sought treatment for three months, but since I'd left so abruptly, I hadn't been able to sit down and explain to anyone what was really going on. I can only imagine what had been said or the rumors that had flown around the office during my absence, but I'm sure they were hoping I was long gone, never to return.

But return I did, and I have vivid memories of that first day back. It was a Monday, and we typically had a staff meeting at 9:00 to kick off the week. So there I go, waltzing in full of hope and positivity, excited to see everyone… and for them to see the new me. I sauntered into the conference room expecting people to rise to a standing ovation, celebrating the great achievement that was my 90 days of sobriety.

Instead, no one stood. No one clapped. In fact, no one even looked up and acknowledged my existence. I mean *zero* people. There had to be twenty people crammed into this little conference room, and *not one of them* would even make eye contact with me.

I felt like a leper. It was so awkward and uncomfortable, like Pig-Pen from the Peanuts comic strip, the kid who always had the cloud of dust hovering around him. Even though *I* felt clean and new, everyone else still saw me as dirty, with dust spewing out of my mouth each time I started to talk.

I spoke a little later in that meeting and addressed the humongous elephant sitting in the room: where I'd been and why. I don't remember exactly what I said, but when I finished, I could immediately tell this was not a group of people who understood much about addiction nor was ready to forgive me. I now understand why my coworkers felt that way and don't hold anything against these fine folks—many of them have since become very supportive during my journey. The point is:

they didn't get it right away, and if I hadn't had a solid support system in place already, that first day back at work could have really taken a toll on my newly discovered emotions.

If you haven't experienced something like this yet, just give it some time. I assure you: early on in your recovery, you will face situations where people treat you very differently. It can be hurtful. It can be embarrassing. Shoot, it can be downright humiliating. Worst of all, it can plant a seed of resentment which, if not properly rooted out and dug up, could blossom into a relapse.

People aren't the only aspect of your life that can cause you stress and anxiety early in your recovery. Life can and will throw a multitude of distractions, disappointments, and dead-ends at your feet, hoping something will trip you up. Your addiction will fight back and wants this stuff to bump you off your recovery or aftercare plans. Awkward reunions, new jobs, running into old using/drinking buddies, facing the holidays sober, financial woes, romantic frustrations... they'll all come along, but they don't have to push you back into negative thinking and behaviors.

Those of you who have already experienced some of these situations know this is easier said than done, right? So how do we counteract these triggers and emotional trials? How do we give ourselves the best shot at maintaining sobriety?

One way is to proactively form a solid team around us we can lean against, one day at a time. As I re-emerged into the world of "normies," one of my main missions was to build that team. It was and still is a diverse group of people from all walks of life that I could go to receive advice, to vent, to seek counsel and in general, support me as I embarked on my most dangerous mission called sobriety.

The truth is, only a very small percentage of people who attempt sobriety are able to make it to the two-year mark. Staying clean and sober in the world we live in is not an easy task; in fact it's incredibly difficult. So to give myself a fighting chance, I sought others in my community who I wanted to walk beside me through this journey.

Guys like Mont S., who has been my sponsor since the first week I checked out of treatment. Mont is a guy who always answers the phone and responds to text messages faster than any human on earth—the guy is like a machine with his iPhone. This may sound like a small detail, but it was really important to me early; when he responded to my questions or cries for help so quickly it made me feel valued and connected,

60

like he genuinely cared about what was going on with me. He didn't know it, but he was giving me courage and filling my tank with confidence I am still running on today. Mont has been incredibly gracious and kind to me. God put him in my life for a reason and I'm so thankful I muttered those words to him: "Will you be my sponsor?"

Jim Riley is another man I count as a part of my team. As I mentioned before, Jim worked with me in the early days and made sure I went to the right treatment center, the one best suited for me and my addiction. Since those early days, Jim has been a part of every big decision I've made, like where I should live or what jobs I should take. He's been there for me during disappointing times, always encouraging and supporting me as a person. He taught me how to work with other addicts and how to be patient. But most importantly, he's been the most *consistent* example of what it means to give back. For close to thirty years now, he and his lovely wife Robin have dedicated their lives to the pursuit of serving others. Jim is a godly and generous man, one I look up to and long to be like.

Spiritual influences are huge part of my accountability circle as well. Pastors like Dr. Hance Dilbeck, Chris Bennett and Israel Hogue have played a major role in my growth as a believer. They've urged me to stay grounded in the scriptures and gave me a living example of what it means to be Christ-like. I look up to these guys in a big way. I bother them for meetings every month just so I can pick their brains on the scripture and glean from their many years of experience leading people to deeper relationships with Christ. These types of spiritual mentoring relationships should also be a huge component of your accountability team. Seek out men or women in leadership positions who know how to handle stress well. In addition to the spiritual bounty you will receive, they will most certainly be able to provide you some good stress management insight as well.

One person I could never leave off my team of supporters is my best friend and number-one fan, Allyson, who has been by my side for years. Ally witnessed firsthand the downfall and destruction my life became during the latter part of my addiction and has, like her mother once described her to me, brought so much light that she's like turning on the light switch in a dark room. She is a kind-hearted and hard-working woman, standing by me as my life tumbled down into nothing and, time and again, begging and pleading for me to get help. Ally suffered through the worst part of me and yet never left my side, and when I *finally* took that first step toward sobriety, she was right there to cheer me on and help me back on my feet. Whether a situation has gone really well or really bad, Ally is the first person I call. Everyone—especially addicts— need an encourager, someone who has your back and loves you just the way you are. Allyson is that person for me; I don't know where I'd be without her.

To round out my Hope Partners, I sought a man who had two things I wanted: creativity and influence. Scott Williams is that man. A former pastor turned social media expert and church consultant, Scott is extremely well-connected and one of the brightest men I've ever known. Once I'd recovered enough to allow my head to begin clearing, I knew I wanted to expand my marketing background and I believed Scott was a person who could help me do that. After bugging him and his assistant for a solid year, I finally got on his schedule.

From our first meeting, Scott graciously answered all my questions and opened up his list of contacts to connect me to anyone he thought could help. We've become fast friends over the past year, and his encouragement is a large reason why I chose to write this book. If it wasn't for me reaching out to

Scott multiple times seeking a mentoring relationship, I would have never fulfilled this bucket-list dream I had to write a book. He gave me the support I needed. Showed me how to do it and then helped me get it done. That's a good mentor. As Tom Pace would say, a good mentor is someone who has been where you want to go and is willing to help you get there as well.

Some of the best gifts God gives to those in recovery are new lifelong friendships; men and women, brothers and sisters who walk alongside you down this narrow road of sobriety. This aspect of my recovery has been one of the most rewarding of experiences. Before I found sobriety, I may have had a couple of people in my life that I could call "friends," and even those guys quit taking my phone calls near the end of my run.

But today that's not the world I live in. I am so blessed to count so many people as good friends. Men like Mark H., Floyd C., Aaron H., Jeremy P., Trey C., Sheridan A., and Shane D. These are the guys I battled alongside for 90 long days to reclaim my life. Or guys like Jeff L., Michael G., Micah A., Jason W., and Sean C., whom I watched as they fought for their freedom during their stint at Rob's Ranch.

I could go on and on listing all the incredible people

I have met along this journey. The key is not simply in the new friendships themselves, but in their depth and meaning. All these men in my life are just short-term acquaintances if I don't allow them to encourage me or build me up, if I don't vulnerably open myself up for their correction and rebuke. These men are my friends, but they are also a part of my team. I need as many people watching me as possible—these guys have walked through the fire with me, so what better people could I have?

Most importantly, when it comes to forming my dream team of supporters, the first two captains I chose were my parents. I knew they had my back from day one of this journey and they have never let me down. They've participated in every counseling session, addiction discussion, or recovery type event I have ever asked them to attend. In fact, as I grew in my sobriety, my parents jumped on the bandwagon in full force. As my Dad would put it, they were "all about recovery." He's a pastor, remember, so he preached multiple sermons about addiction recovery and came and taught Bible studies to the guys at Rob's Ranch when I was their Executive Director. He filled my head with great ideas about how to raise awareness about addiction. He became a big advocate for the recovery movement.

As for my Mom, all she did was send me motivational emails that included detailed spiritual application every day I was in treatment. Yes, you read that right. Every. Single. Day. *That's* how great a mother she is. Her dedication to me and her willingness to learn about what I was going through during those months will stay with me forever. What a marvelous and beautiful woman!

My parents have been there for me during these first couple of sober years, but more importantly than just having them there, I wanted them to know that I needed their help, guidance, and maybe most notably, their *correction*. I gave my parents full permission to ask me anything they wanted. If there was a question about something I was doing, any item I was buying, or even where I was headed, they could grill me all they wanted. Trust me: this was a dramatic swing in our relationship. Prior to getting sober, I was one secretive son-of-a-gun. I never let *anyone* know my full plans or intentions. But as I sobered up, I knew that old way of doing things had to go, that I had to open up my life and let in those who cared about me the most.

Something to Think About

Think about this as you begin forming of your own team: how many great athletes, musicians, or cultural leaders had incredible teams supporting them?

Without Brian Epstein and George Martin we would have never known John, Paul, George, and Ringo as the collective cultural phenomenon that we do today. Brian Epstein, whom Paul McCartney called "the fifth Beatle," took those four mop-tops from Liverpool and molded them into a professional act. He paid for their first LP himself and shopped it to nearly every record company in London before finally meeting up with producer George Martin. Martin went on to offer the Beatles their first record contract without ever having met them or hearing them play live. The rest is history.

What about LeBron James? How many NBA titles did he win prior to joining up with Dewayne Wade and Chris Bosh in Miami? Zero would be the answer. He got close a couple times while playing with the Cleveland Cavaliers, but in the end he couldn't get over the hump because the team around him wasn't built properly to support him. Even after he landed in South Beach things didn't all just fall into place. It wasn't until his second year and the addition of defensive stopper Shane Battier, the maturation of role players like Mario Chalmers, and the re-emergence of three-point specialist Mike Miller did LeBron finally capture that elusive championship ring.

Successful individuals are surrounded by solid teams.

You need this in your life as well. You don't have to be a songwriting genius or a stud athlete to have a great team around you. Don't let anyone tell you or make you think your life isn't worth having the best supporters, encouragers, and correctors this world has to offer. You only have one life; make it exceptional!

Still not convinced? Think about it in this way. What do all great companies or organizations have? Good lawyers, solid accountants, dedicated sales teams, creative marketers, and visionary leaders. Successful entities are made up of diversely skilled people who all come together to make a product or service the best it can be. In this case, you are that product, and your life is worth having a good team in place to help you be all you can be.

For the sake of this book, call these men and women in your life your "Hope Partners." If you are actively in AA or NA, then include your sponsor. If you don't have a sponsor, get one. If you are in Celebrate Recovery or any other recovery-based program, you should include your mentor or someone from that group on your team. But be careful not to just pick from one pool of potentials. Stretch yourself, put yourself out there, and seek people who have something you really want.

Maybe they have a story of addiction or a trauma in their past that's similar to yours, so you see their recovery as inspiring and motivational. That's great! You want them on your team!

Maybe they've been successful in business since they've sobered up and that piques your interest. Go after them!

Maybe you're attracted to the balance in the life of a fellow recovering addict. Their life seems to be one you'd like to mimic. Sounds like they are another good choice!

Maybe you desire their spiritual life and they seem to have a lot of insight they could share. Perfect! That's a great person to have on your team!

Maybe a man or woman in your life is really well-connected and could possibly open doors to new opportunities. You definitely will need someone like him or her during those first few years, so get them on your side!

As you work through the challenge at the end of this chapter and write down your prospective Hope Partners, I encourage you to stretch yourself outside of the "recovery" community. If you noticed as I discussed my team of Hope Partners, not all of them were recovering addicts. That was by choice.

Why? For starters, I spent a year living and working at a treatment center, engrossed daily in all things addiction, therapy, and the like. I needed to balance my life with a set of mentors who walked in different circles. Men and women who could not only pour into me encouragement and inspiration, but who could also help me achieve some of the goals I had set as a newly sober man.

As you will read in the spiritual application section of this chapter, the principle and perks of maintaining strong mentors have been around for centuries. Most of the successful people this world has seen have made it a priority to seek out and surround themselves with inspirational and influential people. These people will help provide you with credibility and confidence as you transition back into mainstream society. They will not only be there to guide you through tough situations, but in the end, you will earn their stamp of approval, and this will prove invaluable as you go about your life.

We've talked about our need to surrender our old ways of doing life. For most of us, that old life included blocks of time spent in seclusion, hidden away from the world. When we did venture out, we maintained a small group of cohorts who typically shared one common denominator: drinking and using.

It's time to make a change. It's time to seek out a diverse set of accountability partners who maintain values, skills, and character qualities you *want* in your life, but that you don't necessarily have yet. It's time to put together your dream team—men and women who will help hold you firm in recovery and propel you into your new, quality life.

It's time to choose your Hope Partners!

CHALLENGE

I cannot over-stress the importance of aligning yourself with a group of stable supporters, mentors who will get to know you and who have permission to call you out and correct you when you need it. There are two steps to this challenge:

1) Identify five people today who you are going to ask to be your Hope Partners. Take some time to think over and pray about these individuals.

Reread some of this chapter if you struggle with determining who those folks might be. Remember, the power lies in your hands. Don't be afraid to seek out strong, influential people. Most successful people want to give back and are just waiting for someone to give them an opportunity to do so. You can't receive if you don't ask!

2) Write down what you are going to say. Develop a strategy for your presentation. Work up a plan outlining how to approach these potential Hope Partners. What do you plan on telling them about yourself? What do you want out of this relationship? Be specific, be intentional, and don't walk in unprepared. I know it's tempting to get frustrated with this part of the exercise; it's not easy to write strategies like this out on paper. Some of you work better on the fly and just speaking from you heart. I get that, and I tend to be more like that as well. But trust me, when you walk up to someone you don't know well with the intentions of asking them to

support you in your journey, you will want to have something prepared.

To help you get started, I've provided a few examples below. Each one is for a different type of partner. Recovery partners, like sponsors, really should be the easiest to approach; after all carrying the message to other addicts is an ingrained piece of most quality programs. But as you branch out into the world of non-addicts, the world's ignorance regarding addiction can make things more difficult.

Read through my examples and use them as starting points to write your list, adjusting it according to your specific addiction or situation. *Please don't skip this part.* It's important you think through what you are going to say to someone when you are asking them to take time out of their life to help protect yours.

Hope Partner Inquiry Example: Recovery

Hi _____, my name is Lance Lang. For the past ten years I have battled with an addiction to alcohol and OxyContin. I've been sober for _____ months/years now and am really looking to take my life to another level. I've watched you in meetings and listened to what you have to say, and I realize you have something that I want. Would you consider coming alongside me and helping me find the joy in recovery that you have found?

Hope Partner Inquiry Example: Spiritual Guidance

Hi _____, my name is Lance Lang. I'm not sure if you know much about my story, but over the past ten years I've battled an addiction to alcohol and OxyContin. This addiction tore my life apart, but thankfully about _____ months/years ago I found sobriety and am working hard to establish a new life.

I've noticed that you seem to have a strong spiritual connection with God. This is something I have struggled with in the past, but is an area in my life I know I need to strengthen. Would there be a time we could grab coffee and I could ask you a few questions about your faith and what's helped you develop it over the years?

Hope Partner Inquiry Example: Business or Industry Professional

Hi _____, my name is Lance Lang. I'm not sure if you know much about my story, but over the past ten years I've battled an addiction to alcohol and OxyContin. This addiction tore my life apart, but thankfully about _____months/years ago I found sobriety and am working hard to establish a new life.

I've noticed that you run a [type of business] and that's something I am very interested in pursuing. I would be honored if one day I could take you out to lunch, tell you a little more about my story, and ask you some questions about how you got where you are today. Would you be willing to meet with me, maybe next week sometime?

Spiritual Application

Hope Partners come in all sizes and flavors. Clearly, a Hope Partner will come alongside you as your draw near to God. Remember, A Hope Partner is not someone who will push you into relapse, but someone who will guide you into a new existence.

In the Bible, Barnabus became a sponsor, a Hope Partner of sorts for the apostle Paul. Paul wrote the majority of the Christian New Testament and planted many of the early churches. However, before that he was a *persecutor* of the church!

Although Paul was called to be an apostle by the will of God, because of his past, his acceptance into the early church community came through the sponsorship or mentorship of Barnabas (see Acts 9:26-30). This relationship was crucial to Paul's advancement into becoming an influential leader of the early Christian church. It was Barnabas, risking his reputation and position as a church leader, who finally persuaded the disciples to accept Paul, making a way to what would be an incredibly world-changing future. Later, Paul passed on the gift Barnabas gave him and sponsored Onesimus as he attempted to reestablish a broken relationship with Philemon. What a beautiful example of passing along what was freely given to Paul.

"As iron sharpens iron, and one man sharpens another." (Proverbs 27:17, ESV)

Bottom line: we need positive partners in our lives to help us reestablish credibility in this world. But it's crucially important to make sure at least one of your Hope Partners has a strong spiritual background. They should be someone who will enlighten and encourage you on your spiritual journey.

CHAPTER 4

GET A ROUTINE

"Your success is determined by your daily agenda"

--John Maxwell

"Whatever you do, work heartily." Colossians 3:23 (ESV)

Ask anyone with a good amount of "sober days" under their belts about a key aspect of their success in early recovery and many will reply: the consistency of solid routine.

I define a "routine" as repetitiously processing through a series of positive actions designed to help you stay focused in your mind, your body, and your spirit.

We all, recovering addicts or not, get caught up in the busy-ness that is life. Whether it's parenting, managing multiple jobs, dating, heading to church functions, going to meetings, getting coffee, performing charity work, doing housework, upholding personal obligations, or any number of other things, we live in a very busy world. If we're not careful, our balance can easily shift so we lean in the wrong direction. For addicts, getting out of balance is a risk we can't afford to take.

But how are we supposed to stay slow and take things one day at a time when everyone else seems to be sprinting toward a bigger and brighter future? The key lies in a solid routine full of quality time with God, an abundance of self-reflection, and a good bit of positive reinforcement.

I understand the natural aversion some addicts have to routine. How long have we lived in a world of doing whatever we wanted, whenever we wanted to do it? This free-spirited mentality may cause some of you to believe that routines will restrict your freedom and limit your ability to grow. The truth is quite the opposite. We set routines to keep us balanced as we seek out that desired freedom and growth. As we re-enter the world as new beings, most experiences will produce emotions and feelings that for years have lain dormant. By setting and sticking to a solid routine, we're solidifying our foundation, enabling us to handle these unfamiliar sensations in a healthy way.

Addiction professionals will tell you that your maturation process, both mentally and emotionally, drastically slows down when you begin drinking and using. For some, this process stops altogether. For example, I was 28 when I got clean. But since I started using when I was seventeen, emotionally I was more like a teenager than a mature adult when I found sobriety.

Transfer that equation to your situation and you begin to comprehend the true challenges the newly sober must face. Our drug or alcohol use, combined with our reckless lifestyle, has hindered our maturation and limited our ability to make good decisions. Furthermore, we've suppressed our emotions for years as well to the point where we are almost childlike. Every day is full of new experiences and new emotions.

We can best handle change if we expect it in the context of a familiar routine. A predictable routine allows us to feel safe and to develop a sense of mastery in handling our new life, reinforced daily. As this happens, we can begin to tackle larger changes in our lives. Wrapping your new and different life within a framework of a solid routine will be critical for your success in the real world.

Here are a few ways routines help us keep hope alive.

Routines provide structure. Routines allow us to tackle new and complex situations in a reliable and protective way. By systematically approaching each day, we begin to develop positive habits and teach our brains to make good decisions. We learn to be consistent, a word seldom used to describe our behavior in the past. Additionally, on slow, boring days—the types of days when we used to make poor decisions—our routines help us stay in the moment. They keep us grounded, tied down to the reality of our situation.

Routines provide self-confidence. As we check off our list every day, our confidence grows. We are accomplishing tasks we never could have completed while drunk or high. As this self-assurance grows, our fear of the unknown begins to slowly diminish and true change seems a little more possible. Courage and self-esteem build within us as we successfully take on new responsibilities.

Routines prepare us for the future. As we practice our routines, innately we will begin to develop skills that will serve us greatly in the days to come. Waking up early, making our bed, finding time to read, and saying prayers before we go to bed all mimic the type of professional schedule we've failed to maintain in the past. Our routine keeps us focused and always looking ahead, inherently building up strategic planning and time-management skills.

Routines boost your spiritual connections. Making a concerted effort to seek God each day will naturally grow your understanding of Him and drive your faith to levels never before attained. As you carve out daily time to consciously contact Him through prayer, mediation, and daily devotionals, God will begin to reveal His truths to you. Momentum will grow as you begin to see how God's sovereign hand has guided and protected you even through your addiction.

Routines produce creativity. When you achieve a balanced and relaxed life, you have easier access to your intuition and creativity. Exercise and enjoying nature can refresh your mind and help you get back to your true self. Within all of us lies a creative being; by maintaining a routine we allow that person the freedom to thrive.

My Routine

I try to start and end my days on my knees. Many of you have been taught this practice or have heard it suggested at church or at meetings. I've found when I started and ended my day on my knees in an act of submission to God,

I was in a much better place throughout the day. I was more compassionate, more caring, and felt more in-tune with what God was doing in and through my life. It's my way of surrendering daily.

In the morning, I literally try to roll out of bed onto my knees. I start first thing by asking God to help guide me and keep me sober throughout the upcoming day. Plopping down on your knees first thing in the morning is not the easiest thing to do. Sometimes you forget or nature's call is just too strong to avoid. Here are a few suggestions to help get you in the habit of starting your days on your knees:

- Put your mobile phone under your bed each night. That way when you get up, you have to squat down to pick it up. Since you are already down on your knees, you might as well say a little prayer!

- Put a sign on the inside of your bedroom door. All it needs to say is "prayer" or "knees." It will act as a subtle reminder of what you need to do before you start preparing for your day.

- If you don't slide your phone under your bed, then set a reminder on your phone that pops up about the time your alarm goes off. All it needs to say is "prayer time."

The second part of my routine is my daily readings. This one is pretty self-explanatory. However, it's important that you find the right books for *you*. There are hundreds of AA and NA daily inspirations, reflections, one-day-at-a-time or 24-hour-type books. There are even more devotional style books from Christian authors like Max Lucado and John Maxwell. A book by Sarah Young titled *Jesus Calling* is one of the most powerful devotional books ever written. I would highly recommend adding it to your list of daily readings.

Another option is to use your computer or mobile device to follow and read inspirational blogs (you can find some at HopeIsAlive.net) or to download the free YouVersion Bible app to instantly have hundreds of custom reading plans at your fingertips; plans for a variety of topics and seasons of life. If you've never read the Bible, this app is a great tool to ease you into it.

The point is, there are thousands of choices, but not all of them are for you. Find two or three daily reading books that fit your personality, spiritual condition, and most importantly, speak to your addiction specifically. Yes, I believe that, regardless of your drug or drink of choice, 100% abstinence from drugs and alcohol is the only way to obtain true sobriety. However, if you have spent most of your time with a needle in your arm or tooter up your nose, then the AA *24 Hours a Day* book is probably not the best reading plan for your recovery. Maybe you should think about an NA alternative.

One more thought on the topic of inspirational books. I try to create a constant environment of learning and growth in all facets of my life, so in addition to recovery-based books and spiritual growth guides, I also add professional growth materials to the mix. That means reading business-based volumes to stay balanced and on top of my work life.

Balance is a key aspect to your entire recovery plan and it's no different when it comes to what you read. For the first few weeks of your recovery, don't worry about this, but as you begin to pick up more and more chips, start broadening your reading to include books about your specific trade or business industry.

As an example, here is what my daily reading looks like:

- *Just for Today* daily devotional by Narcotics Anonymous

- *Jesus Calling* by Sarah Young
- *Go Big!* by Scott Williams

(And don't forget you can always read through the big book or the Bible!)

The third aspect of my routine (and one I am particularly fond of) is meditation and exercise. I combine these activities in my daily routine because they work hand-in-hand.

As an addict in recovery, I still have strong tendencies toward depression, anxiety, and general discontentedness. One remedy I have found to help counteract some of this negative mental activity is scheduling time during my work day to achieve balance. If at all possible, I try to make time to meditate and exercise in the middle of my day. I have a membership at a local gym where I try to hit the treadmill a few times a week. I discovered very early on in my recovery process how much I actually enjoyed running. It's a great way to clear your mind and an easy, cheap, healthy way to still get high (runners' high, that is!).

Recently I also discovered yoga. What a mind-blower that was! I love the balance and meditation time that yoga affords my life. I prefer going to a "hot" yoga studio, where the room temperature is between 95-100 degrees. Boy, it gets hot in there, but I love feeling the sweat pouring off my body, a tangible reminder of all the junk I'm cleaning out of my system every day.

Not only is hot yoga a hardcore workout that helps flexibility and strengthens that gut you abused for so long, but it also forces you to look inward. You are constantly challenged to control your breathing or to focus on certain areas of your body as you work them. Your mind works overtime—and we all need that. Typically yoga classes incorporate 10-15 minutes of meditation as well, so you can kill two birds with one stone. You get the awesome, sweat-filled workout your body needs and then end the class by taking some time to reflect on your day, your attitudes, and your actions.

The final piece of my exercise puzzle is playing recreational team sports. I play indoor soccer or basketball with other recovering addicts a couple of times a week. I'm a sucker for competition, so this helps me scratch that itch while allowing me to fellowship with other addicts. This helps keep us all in line and out of trouble.

You might be thinking, *Wow, this guy is crazy-busy,* and in some ways I am. But I also know myself well enough to know that having too much down time with nothing to do is *not* a good thing for me. When my life slows down too much, my emotions tend to transfer from my heart to my head, and once I get in my head too long, it quickly becomes a dangerous place.

Understanding yourself, your temperaments, and tendencies is very important when planning your routine. You might not need to stay as active as I do, or you might need to make yourself *more* active. Or maybe you do, but you don't have the money to join a gym or attend yoga classes. That's all right. Run, walk, or meditate as you stroll through a park or jog around a body of water. All these activities are free of charge and are great ways to seek balance through meditation and exercise.

The fourth aspect of my daily routine includes a purposeful pause to reflect on my actions and interactions with others. This personal inventory moment allows me to step back and review my progress and my state of mind. If need be, I will call myself out when I need to improve, or give myself a pat on the back when I feel I've done something right.

In addition, I take time to encourage myself throughout the day as well. I know this may sound quirky or weird to some of you, but I am a big believer in positive reinforcement.

Granted, I am by nature an encourager to others; this comes very easy to me. But I have to work at and practice talking myself up, with thoughts likes these...

- *You're on the right track; keep moving!*
- *God created you for this moment; you can do this!*
- *Don't let anyone out-work you today.*
- *Look how far you've come in such a short period of time!*
- *I believe in you!*

Or I will recite verses over and over in my head...

- *"For God did not give us a spirit of fear but of power and love and self-control." (2 Timothy 2:7)*
- *"Trust in the Lord with all your heart and lean not on your own understanding; in all your ways submit to him, and he will make your paths straight." (Proverbs 3:5-6)*
- *"If God is for us who can be against us?" (Romans 8:31)*

There have certainly been times when I've practiced this routine better than others. When I've done a good job of maintaining my solid routine, I've seen benefits. Conversely, when my emotions have gotten out of whack or my ego started to rear its ugly head, I can typically trace it back to getting off my daily routine.

It's not easy to stay on a schedule in today's world when we have so many distractions vying for our attention. For recovering addicts, as we fight to change our lives and escape from our old vicious and destructive routines, we must stay disciplined and focused. We must buckle down and secure a solid, consistent routine and stick with it. It's critical for our state of mind, our soul, our spirit, and our sobriety.

Before we get into our challenge for this chapter, read once more through this simplified version of my routine and see if it could help you stay focused throughout your daily living:

1) **Start your day on your knees with prayer.**
   - Begin each morning thanking God for another day.
   - Ask for protection, guidance and wisdom.
   - This is a great act of surrender, physically acknowledging that you are not God and thus you have great need of Him.

2) **Read.**

- Daily devotionals
- Big book or Bible
- Inspirational blogs

3) **Meditate and exercise.**

- Take a moment to center yourself before you leave your house, before you get out of your car, before you start work.
- Yoga, running, walking: all great cardio activities that give you time to think, keep you healthy, and balance your life naturally.
- You need to take time to acknowledge where you are each day and mediation allows you the stillness in which to do so.

4) **Speak over yourself words of encouragement, power, love.**

- Be your biggest encourager. If you won't, who will?
- Speak a mandate over your day. Claim the victory before it happens.
- Get yourself excited to take on life. "Suit up and show up." It's *your* life!

5) **End your day on your knees with prayer.**

- Thank God for another day sober.
- Thank God for another day employed, married, healthy, with family, etc.
- We all have plenty to say thanks for so make a habit of doing it every night.

This routine is crucial for me to follow if I want to stay focused, if I want to stay thankful, if I want to stay sober, if I want to keep on living…

CHALLENGE

What about you? Do you have a routine?

What do you do to stay grounded?

What do you do to stay sober, to stay positive, and to stay on task?

Your routine may look similar to mine; or maybe it's completely different. Either way, I would highly suggest you bookend it with prayer time on your knees, in the morning and at the end your day. There is nothing more important than this.

Take a moment to yourself. Turn on your favorite song. Jot down the positive aspects of your day-to-day activities.

91

What are those all-important components to your recovery that you know you need to make a daily habit? What helps you to stay balanced and in the moment?

Now think about what you need to do...

Write down your routine here. List at least five things. Leadership guru John Maxwell affirms this point in what he calls the Power of Five. He states, "To get what you want, you have to do five things and do them every day."

Your recovery routine:

1.

2.

3.

4.

5.

Spiritual Application

"So do not worry, saying, 'What shall we eat?' or 'What shall we drink?' or 'What shall we wear?' For the pagans run after all these things, and your heavenly Father knows that you need them. But seek first his kingdom and his righteousness, and all these things will be given to you as well.

Therefore do not worry about tomorrow, for tomorrow will worry about itself. Each day has enough trouble of its own." – *Matthew 6:31-34 (NIV)*

Scores of books have been written about time management. I have found that highly successful people in the recovery world have discovered reproducible principles of life; even Jesus gave a tremendous example of consistency and routine when we see that his life was marked by rising early to pray daily. Educators will tell you that repetition has great value. Songwriters know the value of repetition, and so do athletes.

Routine in life reveals what we value. If it's true that we succeed in what we celebrate, then let's get on board and celebrate routines that will foster daily sobriety. Nothing will benefit us more than a daily dose of prayer, Bible reading, and meditation.

But all the routine in the world won't help you if you don't prioritize it first, and your number-one priority, according to Jesus, is to seek God's kingdom first and foremost. Before you take care of what you're going to eat or drink or wear, you need to seek God.

When you make your relationship with God your first priority, then everything else in your routine falls into place! When you learn to trust Him with *every* part of your life, then all those parts seem a little less worrisome.

Let the kingdom of God fill your view.

CHAPTER 5

MAKE A MANDATE

"My self-imposed mandate is to be the voice for the voiceless."

--Dionne Warwick

"The end of all things is at hand; therefore be self-controlled
and sober-minded for the sake of your prayers."

−1 Peter 4:7 (ESV)

Mandate:

1. A command or authorization to act in a particular way.

2. An authoritative order.

3. To authorize or decree

"I Will Not Use, No Matter What!"

I wrote that phrase in my lecture notebook during my

stay at Rob's Ranch, and I still remember the exact moment I wrote it. A feeling of strength came over me as I made a personal mandate that I was done with my old way of living. This statement has pulled me out of many traps the past few years; countless times this personal agreement with myself motivated me to make the right decision in a circumstance that could have proven to be very dangerous.

For instance, there was the time I took off by myself (not something I would suggest early in recovery) on a camping trip to Roman Nose State Park near Yukon, Oklahoma (yes that is actually the name of *both* those places). I was looking forward to this trip—just me and Mother Nature for an entire week. I was convinced I would spend the time sitting outside my RV, writing, reading books, and enjoying the scenery, undisturbed for days.

Well, I tend to forget details and get stuck in the broad picture of things and that's what happened that weekend. I was so focused on packing the right stuff, getting out there, and getting set up that I totally forgot the date.

It was 4th of July weekend.

Now, I am not a complete idiot. I had realized it was a holiday week, I just didn't realize everyone would stay at the state park the *entire* weekend! Next thing I knew, I was surrounded by thirty other RVs full of people partying and partying hard.

So there I was, all alone, stuck in between what sounded like some pretty quality parties. I had no accountability (first mistake) and nowhere I needed to be for days. I have to admit I had some pretty troubling thoughts that first night. But each time my mind wandered into a thought like *No one will ever know* or *You can have a few beers, what's it gonna hurt?* something would click inside my head and I would immediately begin to speak my mandate quietly to myself.

That weekend, saying "I Will Not Use, No Matter What!" became a habit that has stuck with me every day since. I made it through that camping trip and came home stronger than ever in my sobriety. While I should never have put myself in that situation in the first place, I view that time as a turning point in my recovery. It was the one of the most tempting times I had experienced, and I came out of it victorious.

I knew I could do it.

It's important to build your recovery on a firm foundation that includes several key aspects. As we've discussed in previous chapters, surrendering daily, establishing routines, and developing a network of accountability or "Hope Partners" are critical. This foundation you are building will act just like old Bubba did in that famous scene in *Forrest Gump*. You know the one I am talking about. Forrest and Bubba have just finished a long, brutal day of being at war in Vietnam, and the rain was pouring down upon them. They plop down in the mud back to back. Old Bubba leans back and says, "Forrest, I'm gonna lean up against you, you just lean right back against me. This way we don't have to sleep with our heads in the mud."

The foundation you're building is what you need to keep your head out of the mud. Time and time again throughout the first few years of your journey through sobriety, you will look to these tools you are building and creating and call them into action when the time comes.

One key to ensuring a strong footing is a strong mandate statement. Like a mission statement that outlines an organization's values and core beliefs, a mandate is a single sentence that draws you back to the core of who you want to be as a person in recovery. Your mandate acts as a barometer or measuring stick for you to gauge your conduct, your decisions, and your reactions, reminding you at crucial moments what's really important to you.

So what is *your* mandate? Have you ever sat down and thought about it? Do you have a statement you live by, something that drives you forward or keeps you on track? Use whatever analogy you would like for your mandate. Call it your rudder, your barometer, your compass, your GPS—whatever you want. Just get one that means something to you and convicts your heart to act. That is the most important facet of a moving mandate. It must have a passion behind it that will stir you to action.

Keys to a good mandate statement:

1) *Keep It Short.* A mandate statement should be between five and ten words *max*; a phrase you can memorize within a few minutes. You want it to be something your brain will immediately turn to at a moment's notice in the heat of battle.

2) *Keep It Specific.* Make your personal mandate attributable to your life experience, addiction, or struggle. It should be a command that will instantly speak to you while pointing to your future.

3) Keep It Singular. A mandate should have meaning behind it that draws you to a certain time in your life or particular emotion you've experienced, acting as a verbal reminder of who you once were and what would happen if you made the wrong choice. It should be uniquely singular to you.

As I have discussed throughout this book, staying sober takes all kinds of motivation, meditation, messages, training, and teaching. God created us all very differently and that's why it takes so many different methods to be successful in keeping people sober. Hearing this was an important message for me. It resonated, it stuck with me, and when I put it into action, it worked.

CHALLENGE

You know what you do and don't have do in order to quit using or drinking, to protect your heart, to keep your eyes pure, to subdue your anger, to live clean. Take some time, turn on some music, meditate for a few minutes, and think hard about what your mandate statement needs to be.

1) Once you've taken some time to really think

about your mandate statement, jot it down on the line below. What's your mandate? Be intentional. This could save your life....

2) Take a moment to pray that God would allow this mandate to settle into your soul. That He would build power around each of these words and that, as you repeat them over and over again, your strength will build. Pray He would cause them to resonate throughout your life so they come quickly to mind whenever trouble or temptations inevitably spring up.

3) Find a Post-It Note or a piece of paper and grab a roll of tape. Write your mandate on it and put it somewhere you'll see it every day. This mandate you have prayed over your life. This powerful message that will guide you throughout your new life. One day at a time.

Spiritual Application

"Fret not yourself because of evildoers;
be not envious of wrongdoers!

For they will soon fade like the grass

and wither like the green herb.

Trust in the LORD, and do good;

dwell in the land and befriend faithfulness.

Delight yourself in the LORD,

and he will give you the desires of your heart.

Commit your way to the LORD;

trust in him, and he will act.

He will bring forth your righteousness as the light,

and your justice as the noonday."

--Psalm 37:1-6 (ESV)

Some, myself included, would call a mandate a confession; I'm a firm believer in confessing our mandate. The Bible says, "out of the abundance of the heart a man speaks." Another verse says, "as a man thinks, so he is."

Here is the deal: what we say reveals who we are. Our mandate reveals our hearts desire, so say what we believe.

I challenge you to confess your mandate to yourself and others *daily*. When you confess your helplessness over your situation, you will better be able to live out your mandate. The sooner a friend hears your mandate, the sooner they can come alongside you in your life quest.

Three words stand out to me in the passage above:

trust, delight, and *commit.*

Trust in the Lord.

Delight in obedience.

Commit to the Lord.

Sounds a lot like a mandate to me.

CHAPTER 6

JUST SAY YES!

"Do whatever he tells you." --John 2:5b

"As I say yes to life, life says yes to me!" –Louise Hay

"Saying yes means getting up and acting on your belief that you can create meaning and purpose in whatever life hands you." –Susan Jeffers

"When we learn to say a deep, passionate yes to the things that really matter, then peace begins to settle onto our lives like golden sunlight sifting to a forest floor."
--Thomas Kinkade

Nancy Reagan probably wouldn't like this chapter.

In 1982, while on a tour of elementary schools in

Oakland, California, the then-First Lady of the United Sates was approached by a young schoolgirl who asked her what she should do if she was offered drugs. The first lady responded by saying, "Just say no." Powerful, huh? Whew... I bet the little girl never ever did drugs... the end.

Somehow, I doubt it. I bet she nodded and ran off to continue recess with very little consideration of the phrase.

The slogan "Just Say No," as catchy as it may be and as helpful as I am sure it is to give young people a quick retort, comes across negative and empty. There is no real action in it, and as we've discussed so far, we need action to stay sober. We need deliberate steps to change our lives.

So although NO is the right answer to any requests to get high and watch *Super Troopers* (again), YES is the answer that's going to keep us sober for the rest of our lives, one day at a time.

Saying NO continually can stop momentum and stymie growth.

Oftentimes when we say NO we're left with awkward tension inside. You can almost feel the battle within as you say the word. Someone asks you to share your story or they seek your availability for a charity event and your response is, "Noooooo, I've got this thing," as you frantically pull out your phone to start fake-checking your calendar. You continue, "Yeah, nooooo I can't, I'm sorry."

Do you hear the tension in the word NO? It's that long, stretched-out response overflowing with anxiety and guilt. It's just a nasty word.

No requires zero follow-up or commitment. In fact, it's a negative phrase that is typically said for no other reason than our own convenience.

Additionally, research shows that 77% of our thoughts are negative and counterproductive. We are perpetually programming our mind to think *NO! NO! NO!* This definitely happens as we begin to gain sobriety. Whether you find yourself in a treatment center, sober living environment, or holed up in your parents' basement until they decide you can re-enter society, the word NO is all around you:

- No, you can't use anymore
- No, you can't see that person
- No, you can't go to that place
- No, that friend is off limits
- No, you can't see your kids
- No, you can't use your phone

While all these things may be justified and needful at times, when it comes to taking action in your recovery, you are in charge. You and you alone determine how successful you will be.

So it's time to claim responsibility and just say YES!

What do I mean by that? Hear me out. *Just say YES* was the tone I took when I began to turn my life around. Today, I credit this action-packed response as one of the single biggest reasons I stayed sober my first year out of treatment and furthermore, why 85% of the rest of my class did not.

No, I didn't say YES to drugs or alcohol. I said YES to anything and everything my Hope Partners asked me to do. When mentors, counselors, pastors, or my sponsor would push me to take a risk and reach out to someone or to try something I had never done before, I would simply say YES. It became my motto for that season of my sobriety and it helped me grow immensely.

After being in treatment for only a few weeks, I was asked to start leading a daily Bible study. What did I say? YES, I can do that.

Soon after I left rehab, I was asked to get up and tell my story at 6:00 am to five men who were barely awake and didn't really want to be there in the first place. So what did I say? YES! I will be there.

Later, I was asked to start leading a men's recovery meeting on Wednesday nights with a bunch of guys, the vast majority of whom had been sober longer than I had. I was nervous, but I said YES!

I could go on and on and on with other times I was asked to do something outside my comfort zone, things that scared me a little… okay, maybe a *lot*. For example, there was the time I was asked to run a treatment center with only six months' sobriety to my credit. Yeah, that one was a little intimidating, but it proved to be exactly what God wanted me to do at the time. All I had to do was say YES and trust Him with the rest.

As I look back, the personal growth and development I experienced during those strenuous times was nothing short of amazing. Each time I took a step of faith and put myself out there, God gave me the courage and strength to get through it.

Rarely did I say all the right things or make it through flawlessly. Those first few times I led the groups at Rob's Ranch were nerve-wracking, getting up in front of all my peers and sweating profusely. It was crazy; I had never done that before, but for whatever reason, my newly found sobriety led me to sweating fits at the worst possible times. It was so embarrassing. But I pushed myself through it, knowing that growth would only come when I stretched myself beyond my typical limits. I had to put myself out there and simply do what I hadn't been doing for years. I had to start saying YES!

As you begin to apply this principle you will see countless doors open.

As you begin saying YES to new and challenging possibilities, you are in essence putting on another protective layer of surrender. With each YES, you admit that your old ways did not work and that you're willing to try something new. Your foundation will strengthen and your footing will become more stable.

Picture it this way: from childhood, our negative experiences and circumstances have produced destructive behaviors and habits. These damaging behaviors and habits are present in our lives as we transition into adulthood. We carry them with us and begin to use them more and more to maintain a sense of safety and survival. But they begin to act like walls building up around us.

Here are some examples of the experiences or

circumstances that produce these negative habits:

- The abandonment you felt as a young child when your parents split.

- The loneliness and heartache of losing a parent during the impressionable pre-teen years.

- The ridicule and humiliation you lived through in high school.

- The divorce in your mid-twenties.

- The unexpected loss of a spouse or child.

- The time you were violated.

- The time you violated someone else.

This painful list could go on and on.

To cope with these painful experiences, you medicate yourself through addictive habits that become the bricks in the wall. Each day, with each drink or hit, the wall builds higher and higher until you're isolated behind it. Alone and depressed.

Now our drinking and using kick in to high gear in hopes of countering these dark feelings that invade us. But it never works. The use just pushes us to retreat further behind the wall until we're living in the shade and seclusion the wall provides.

Some of us never find our way out.

Some of us die behind this wall.

Is that the life you want? Trapped behind a wall?

Of course not. No one really wants that. For many of you, just reading those few paragraphs took you back to a really dark place. For that I am sorry. My dark place isn't one I prefer to visit often, either. However, if we don't take the necessary action to destroy that wall, it prevents anything good from coming in and, possibly more damaging, stops anything from going *out*.

That is where we'll end up.

Trapped.

Alone.

So how do we destroy this wall?

We say YES!

- YES to surrendering daily.
- YES to a routine.
- YES to your mandate statement.

YES is a response that acts as a change agent; that's what we're looking for, right? Change? Each time you say YES, you're tearing down a piece of that wall you so careful built up around you while you were using, the wall you guarded so closely to keep everyone at a distance.

As you say YES to helping others or to forgiving someone from your past or to any positive action your Hope Partners suggest, it's as if you're taking a huge sledge hammer to that wall and smashing a few more bricks out of it. The more you do this, the stronger you become. The harder you start whipping that hammer, the more bricks fall. Pretty soon the wall is low enough for you to see over it. Wow, what a view! It's a whole new world out there; one you never knew existed, waiting for you on the other side of the wall.

As the bricks tumble to your feet, you realize the trash of the past, the stuff you've hidden behind for so long, can now be recycled into fuel for your new life. One by one, as you take action and say YES to new experiences and overcoming past fears, the bricks begin to almost magically slide under your feet, bolstering your foundation, elevating you higher and higher, where your voice can be heard by more and more people. Soon your foundation is stronger than it's ever been and your influence is stretched wider than ever. The more you say YES, the more your confidence grows and the more accountability you have.

Now, questions are rising in some of your minds as you read this, so let me take a moment and clarify a few points.

First of all, I am not saying your answer to everything that is asked of you should be YES.

Let me repeat: *I am not saying that you must say YES to anything anyone asks of you!*

I am, however, assuming that by now you have established a core group of people to hold you accountable, that at some level you've engaged in a recovery process that's provided you with a pool of qualified individuals to surround yourself with over the next few years. These people, spiritual leaders, and possibly your family, should encompass the team of accountability we call Hope Partners. Hope Partners are a must-have (see chapter two).

Once those supporters are in place and you've taken time to meet with them and have heart-to-heart conversations, then and only then do you put this principle into practice.

As addicts, we are prone to please people and tend to drift toward co-dependency. Consequently, we need to tread carefully when it comes to what—or who—we say YES to. But if we stay focused and have picked the right Hope Partners, then the requests that come our way are necessary and ultimately beneficial.

On the other hand, putting your trust in the hands

of outsiders can be a challenge. It's a scary proposition and one you might choose to skip. *I urge you not to.* Because it's within the realms of those meaningful relationships and the action they produce that real change takes place. I know it's something you haven't done in years. But anything worth doing doesn't come easy. So take action, take a risk, and make a change.

What happens if a person outside our pocket of Hope Partners asks us to do something? Simple answer: call up one of your partners and discuss it. You'll both know the right answer in short order. Typically, if it's a worthwhile request and one that will push you to grow emotionally, physically, or spiritually then the answer should be YES!

By pushing you onward and upward, your sobriety will be strengthened. Furthermore, saying YES intrinsically provides value to your life in other areas:

1) *A YES will feel good.* The more you open yourself up to the idea of saying YES, the more you'll begin to realize how much you enjoy it. The feelings that accompany triumphing over past fears are exhilarating. Even those who don't love change would agree that, by staying

in the same routine day after day, saying NO to invitations and NO to offers, is pretty unlikely to lead you to anything new or different. Follow me on this. Say NO out loud three times. How did that feel? By the third time you probably were frowning. Think about it... Now, say YES out loud three times... go. Say it again. You're smiling aren't you? Gotcha!

2) *A YES will open doors to new opportunities.*
Have you seen the movie *Yes Man*? If you have, you know just how powerful a YES can be when it comes to finding unexpected opportunities. If you don't say YES sometimes, you're missing out on things you don't even know you're missing out on. In the movie, the main character, Carl, finds opportunities in all sorts of wild places, all because he said, you guessed it: YES. Of course, not every YES will lead to something wonderful and unexpected, but you never know what lies on the other side of YES. Maybe it's a new job, a new relationship, a newfound talent, a new friendship, a new hobby.

115

These opportunities are knocking on our front doors, but we must take the initiative and say YES. We must open the door.

3) *A YES helps you overcome fear and insecurity.* Do you know the main reason why most people say NO? Fear. We're scared. We're crippled by the thought of what new people might ask of us or what new experiences may require of us. Our walls have kept us secluded for so many years that our mind has tricked us into thinking we won't enjoy new practices or that we'll look silly if we decided to try. What will people think? What will they say? Those bricks of insecurity and fear must be demolished. We must face them head on! Just remember: with every YES, the bricks of fear and insecurity are falling and a firm foundation of freedom is being built!

4) *A YES brings new relationships.* If you're like me, when you were drinking and drugging you had very few true relationships. Friends were few and far between. One of the greatest

gifts sobriety can give you is the restoration of true meaningful relationships. Saying YES is the first vulnerable step to get you there. A YES to attending a new meeting could be the connection point for a lifelong friendship. A YES to a church event could be the setting of your "how I met your mother" story you tell your future children. You never know who will be on the other side of that YES.

CHALLENGE

It bears repeating. You never know what lies on the other side of a YES! New opportunities could be waiting for you, new strengths could be found, and by taking on new and challenging experiences, you will gain momentum to keep your hope alive.

Over the next several months, as you meet with your Hope Partners, I challenge you to say YES to whatever they ask you to do. You've chosen these people, and they've accepted this challenge, so trust them and trust the process. Here are some YESes to get you started. As you read through this list, if one of these pricks your heart, circle it. The next time these opportunities come, you'll know what to say.

- YES – I will take on a leadership position in my recovery group or clubhouse.
- YES – I will share when I am called on tonight.
- YES – I will go to the gym with my buddy who is always asking me to go.
- YES – I will give to my church.
- YES – I will forgive a family member who really hurt me.
- YES – I will stick with my routine that keeps me balanced.
- YES – I will reach out to that friend who I know is hurting.
- YES – I will make time for my children today.
- YES – I will call my parents.
- YES – I will find the Hope Partners I know I need in my life.
- YES – I will go make the amends my sponsor has been asking me to make.
- YES – I will go to a counseling session.
- YES – I will help another addict/alcoholic in need.

- YES – I will go to church this weekend.

- YES – I will start eating better.

- YES – I will stop looking at porn.

- YES – I will pray for others.

- YES – I will do the next right thing.

Just say YES!

Spiritual Application

"On the third day there was a wedding at Cana in Galilee, and the mother of Jesus was there. Jesus also was invited to the wedding with his disciples. When the wine ran out, the mother of Jesus said to him, 'They have no wine.' And Jesus said to her, 'Woman, what does this have to do with me? My hour has not yet come.' His mother said to the servants, 'Do whatever he tells you.'" –John 2:1-5 (ESV)

I love this story. In a couple different ways, it describes a perfect just say YES moment. The setting was a wedding reception at a city called Cana of Galilee. As you read, the host had run out of wine to serve. So when the servants came to Mary the mother of Jesus with this dilemma, she instantly looked at her son with that "I need you to do something about this" look. I can only imagine Jesus' reaction. He knew exactly what she wanted Him to do and He also knew he was capable of doing it. But He didn't feel quite ready yet. Maybe He was nervous; a little scared even. Feelings us addicts can really relate to.

Whatever it was, you can tell by His response that he wasn't initially willing to say yes. I would guess that there was a bit of a pause as Mary looked at her son. She believed in Him, even more so: she needed Him. After a few seconds, I can see Jesus nodding to his mother affirming her request. Saying YES, even for Jesus, was hard. But He did it.

At the moment His headed nodded, I bet Mary quickly turned to the servants and uttered that line: "Do whatever he tells you to do." Indeed, obedience was the order of the day. The servants said YES and did whatever Jesus asked them to do the rest of the afternoon. The miracle would soon follow, thus initiating Jesus' public ministry.

When you say YES to God you are saying YES to obedience. When you say YES to God's plan for your life, you will better be able to say YES to others. My grandfather used to say, "God has a plan for every man, and a grace for every race." Say YES!

120

CHAPTER 7

KEEP THE PEACE

"There is no peace for the wicked." --Isaiah 48:22

"Be diligent to preserve the unity of the spirit and the bond of peace." --Ephesians 4:3

"If possible, so far as it depends on you, be at peace with all men." --Romans 12:18

"If we have no peace, it is because we have forgotten that we belong to each other."
--Mother Teresa

"If you want to make peace with your enemy, you have to work with your enemy. Then he becomes your partner."
--Nelson Mandela

Disappointments will always be a part of life, but the way we deal with disappointment during the early stages of recovery can be dangerous. Arguments, unmet expectations, and deceit can stir up a swell of old emotions that, if you're not careful, can send you back out in a hurry. So what you do when the same old people who twisted you up inside when you were using and abusing start to affect you again? How do you handle the anxiety-ridden situations that drove you to drink in the first place?

What are you going to do the next time you get disappointed?

One answer, and certainly the one which might come most naturally to us, is to deal with the issue, no matter what it is, the way we used to. That picture looks different for all of us, but I venture to guess the picture is still as clear for you as it is for me.

I know what I used to do.

That mental picture is vibrant and horrifying every time it plays in my head. I would run, hide, and use, then hit the repeat button and do it again and again and then again. My desperate retreat from disappointments and pain drove me to seek shelter and solitude in countless hotels, where no one was watching me; that isolation led me to believe I wasn't hurting anyone. *I just need a break,* I'd tell myself. *I'm too stressed at home; let me just take a night to myself.* Stupid, huh?

I didn't know any better at the time. I mean I knew deep down that what I was doing was wrong, just like I'm sure you did. But those emotions brought about by disappointment, rejection, dismissal, or betrayal were buried so far down that, when they did creep back up, even just for an instant, I sprinted away from them with every ounce of energy I could muster.

Any time I had to face disappointment, my emotions drove me to a reclusive state where I would eat and snort as many pills as I could possibly handle, all while furthering myself from any feelings with each high. By the time the run would be over, there was no anger, no guilt, no shame, no pain, and certainly no conviction remaining. I was empty, hollow, and soon would be in need of yet another high to keep the feelings as far away as possible.

We all deal with disappointments and grief in our own ways, yet when we get together and talk about them, they are eerily similar and equally depressing. None of us want to go back to those lost and lonely times—we all want to live the happy, joyous, and free life we've heard so much about. But sometimes life just isn't fair and for addicts, disappointments during the first couple years of sobriety can be excruciating and present a steep uphill battle. So how do we stay in the positive and avoid the spiral so many others haven't been able to avoid?

If you're a Big-Book-thumper, then you grab on to that first step and claim your powerlessness and walk away. But what if the admission of having no power just isn't enough? What if you need action, a plan? Personally, I need a series of tangible steps at my fingertips, available to implement immediately upon the trigger of disappointment.

Relapse is waiting to happen every day; it's creeping behind every corner just waiting to pounce on us. But relapse is lurking even more so in moments of weakness brought about by disappointments, unmet expectations, or even tragedy. It's in the aftermath of those moments where we are most susceptible. Resentments can cement themselves in our hearts and, if we aren't careful, will set up until we sink into discontentment, unhappiness, and lack of fulfillment.

The fact is, this stuff doesn't mystically go away upon reaching some magic length of sobriety. I wish it did, but it doesn't. As much as the journey of recovery produces a much kinder, more compassionate, and caring individual, the unfortunate truth of the matter is: the rest of the world is *not* on the same journey we are. Many still lie, cheat, steal, and manipulate for selfish reasons.

Sound familiar?

So that's enough on the negative. You get the picture. Even when you're in the midst of changing your life and doing so much good, life can still bring a lot of hurt and pain.

The good news is, we can continue to live a life of freedom and peace even in the midst of disappointment. We don't have to go back to those scary places and crazy faces! The peace and serenity you've either experienced in your early days of sobriety or that you can recall from your childhood can be maintained or recaptured.

Guard Your Heart

Think of your life as a beautiful, peace-filled mansion. A place where you feel at ease, serene, and comfortable. It's taken you a long time to build this mansion. Many years of heartache, legal trouble, and battered relationships have tried to stop you from building it, but you finally did it. You worked hard, tried some new tactics, and were able to construct a place where you finally feel at peace.

125

But every morning you look out the window and see robbers waiting outside, just hoping to catch you at a weak moment so they can invade your mansion and steal your peace. They want some of it for themselves or worse yet, they can't stand to see anyone else with it because they've never attained it. That's sad and unfortunate for them, but *their lack of peace has nothing to do with you.*

Sometimes we have to be a little selfish in recovery. We can't give away peace until we learn to keep it ourselves.

So how do we maintain? How do we keep our mansion and not throw it away the first time we step out into the world? Here are three quick tips. Read these carefully—you'll be using this information in the challenge to follow.

> *1) Name the robber.* Understanding and identifying who and what robs you of your peace is the first step towards maintaining it. We must force ourselves to recognize what circumstances cause us to fear, have anxiety, be disappointed or hurt. We need to name the individuals who evoke feelings we aren't fully capable of dealing with yet.
>
> *2) Pursue the robber.* The next step to maintain

peace is to remove the risk of future disappointments. We are trying to be proactive about our recovery, proactive about our peace, proactive about our state of mind. We all want to be successful, and this is just another way to engage the environment around us before *it* engages *us*. The more accountability and protective measures we can put into place, the more likely we will make the right decisions during important crossroads in our recovery.

3) *Disarm the robber.* Some of you have robbers in your life who need some special attention. Pursuing them or distancing yourself from the situation just won't be enough. Maybe you have family member you must learn to live with or a co-worker who's not going anywhere anytime soon. For these robbers, you need to deal with them head-on; meet them in the front yard, so to speak. We will discuss how to do this more in the challenge, but it won't require a weapon, so leave that in the house.

CHALLENGE

And now comes the time to determine how you will keep the peace. First, write down two or three people who are *most likely* to disappoint you or rob you of your peace. These should be people who are actually in your life today—not old users or drinking buddies who should be long gone, but people with whom you will engage. Write their names in the spaces below:

1. _____

2. _____

3. _____

Second, write down two or three situations, events, or circumstances that are most likely to disappoint you or rob you of your peace over the next year. These could be family events on the horizon (like reunions or holiday events), future court dates, upcoming job searches, the stress of moving, or even the likely loss of a loved one. Again, use the spaces below:

1. _____

2. _____

3. _____

Now that you have your two lists, I want you to totally exclude these people and situations from your life forever.

Ha ha! Just joking!

Seriously, go back up to your lists and, next to each entry, write down the name of one of your Hope Partners from chapter two.

Why? As we discussed in chapter six, living in recovery cannot be done alone. It will not happen without companionship and camaraderie. You need individuals who will partner with you as you begin a brand-new life full of future disappointments, people who care enough about you to keep you in line and hold you to your commitments when your world once again feels like it's falling apart.

So now it's time to call your Hope Partners and discuss your lists with them. Tell them what happens to you when you get disappointed by the people and situations you've identified. You need to tell them the ways you've reacted when these situations have occurred in the past. Tell them how you feel physically, emotionally, mentally, everything. If the event hasn't taken place, tell your partner how you used to feel in similar situations and why you chose to list that particular person, event, or situation.

Give them examples of what you used to do when you would get disappointed or hurt. Be specific. Did you run away?

Did you hurt others? Did you use (I am sure you did)? Did you get sick to your stomach? Depressed? Whatever happened, lay it out in detail to your Hope Partners and ask them if it's okay for you to call or text them if this ever happens again. Of course they will say yes.

Why do this? Why tell them how you feel? Because feelings—both physical and emotional—are great tip-offs that something is going on that is dangerous for you.

I know exactly what mine are. Let give you an example. My "people" list includes an ex-girlfriend. The feelings I experienced when she used to disappoint me (and everyone disappoints you sometimes) were loss of appetite, anxiety, and then depression. The feeling in the pit of my stomach was rarely, if ever, replicated by any other person's actions or circumstances. This is how debilitating this *relationship* was to my addiction. Not *her* as a person mind you, but the *way* in which the *relationship* affected me. So for me to stay sober, I had to—and still need to, on occasion—deal with those feelings of disappointment that come from that relationship.

Interestingly enough, the feelings still come back, sometimes in crazy ways, even though that relationship ended long ago. But when they do, I call one of my Hope Partners,

130

tell him what happened and how I am feeling, and let him talk me through it.

Perhaps now you're saying, "Wait, Lance—if she is not in your life, then why did you write her down?" Well, because we're still friends and are slowly rebuilding our relationship. You may find yourself in a similar situation—if you were married or engaged during your addiction, there's a good chance that person is still in your life in some form or fashion.

For over two years now, this ex-girlfriend and I have remained friends and stayed in contact, but when I face times of disappointment about our past relationship, I call a good pastor friend of mine, one of my Hope Partners. He helps keep my mind and my heart grounded. He helps me keep the peace.

Additional Challenge

If, after identifying a person who causes disappointment in your life and working with your Hope partner to overcome it, you still find yourself trapped with dangerous feelings, here is an additional step to help you make—and keep—peace.

But this one is a wee bit challenging because it requires you to meet with the person face to face, or at the very least to talk with them on the phone (no texting allowed). Use this tip with your best discretion. If, for example, you are not legally allowed to be within a hundred feet of this person, then don't go knocking on their door. Be smart about it. Don't use such restrictions as an excuse not to attempt it—just get creative.

Here's the challenge: sit down with each person, knee to knee, look them in their eyes, and tell them this or something like it.

"(insert name), I want you to know that I *(love, respect, admire)* you and I really appreciate you. As you know I am *(trying to get clean, maintain my sobriety, and overcome an addiction*) and a part of that process is learning how to keep peace in my life and deal with relationships that cause me to get unbalanced. I don't make good decisions when I get that way and I can't afford to make any more poor decisions. With that said, in the future if I feel an emotion or sense a trigger coming on based on our relationship, I will distance myself from you. Please understand that if this happens, it's the best thing I can do to maintain peace in my life and therefore remain sober. Again, the goal is to stay balanced and proactively take steps to ensure I make good sound decisions in the future. I really hope that you will understand if we get to that point in this relationship."

Whew! That's a tough one, I know, but here is why you take that risky step: In this exercise you are not engaging them in a conversation. In fact, you may let them know that before you start. What you are doing is strictly verbalizing your emotions and being vulnerable. Vulnerability is a beautiful thing when done in the proper setting. If you come to them with an open heart and an open mind then your vulnerability will shine through. Most of the time the person you are engaging will respect you for your honesty and immediately pledge to support you and do all they can to help you. They might even go so far as ask what they could do to be a part of the solution.

If they don't, what have you lost? Nothing, really. But you've gained confidence and peace of mind, and have taken tangible steps to keep peace in your life.

Spiritual Application

Bill Hybels, Pastor of Willow Creek Community Church outside of Chicago, said this about the need for reconciliation: "The mark of community is not the absence of conflict but the presence of a reconciliatory spirit." As we seek after this spirit in our lives, God begins to bring about peace in what used to be chaotic and volatile relationships. By taking action towards reconciliation, we become the change agent God uses to restore not only our personal relationships, but also people's relationships with Him.

Here are a few ways we can pursue this reconciliatory sprit:

Pray. "You have heard that it was said, 'You shall love your neighbor and hate your enemy.' But I say to you, Love your enemies and pray for those who persecute you." Matthew 5:43-44 (ESV)

Be Gracious. "But love your enemies, do good to them, and lend to them without expecting to get anything back. Then your reward will be great, and you will be children of the Most High, because he is kind to the ungrateful and wicked." Luke 6:35

Believe the truth. Jesus said, "He who does not follow me, cannot be my disciple." God sent His Son, the Prince of Peace, to make peace in this world. He sends His sons and daughters, you and me to make peace.

We read in Proverbs 16:7 what the result of peacemaking can be: "When a man's ways please the Lord, He makes even his enemies to be at peace with him."

134

There is no doubt that coming off years of addiction, I had some enemies. I imagine you do, too. But the Bible makes it clear that peace is attainable, and that formerly volatile relationships can be restored. All I'm saying is... *give peace a chance.*

CHAPTER 8

GIVE IT AWAY, GIVE IT AWAY,

GIVE IT AWAY NOW

"Each one must give as he has decided in his heart, not reluctantly or under compulsion, for God loves a cheerful giver." –2 Corinthians 9:7 (ESV)

"In all things I have shown you that by working hard in this way we must help the weak and remember the words of the Lord Jesus, how he himself said, 'It is more blessed to give than to receive.'" –Acts 20:35 (ESV)

You know that song "Give It Away," by the Red Hot Chili Peppers? For years I didn't know what it was all about. Quite frankly, I found it rather annoying, since I'm much more of an "Under the Bridge" or "Soul to Squeeze" kind of guy. But recently I picked up lead singer Anthony Keidis's autobiography, *Scar Tissue*, and found out the meaning behind the song. Turns out it's about recovery and the consistent message woven throughout most programs created for addicts like us.

The principle states that, by giving away what sobriety, the program, or what others within those confines have given to you, you become more empowered to maintain it. In a nutshell, it means the more we get out of ourselves and freely give back to others, the stronger we become.

Paring it down even further, the Big Book of Alcoholics Anonymous says it like this: "Practical experience shows that nothing will so much insure immunity from drinking as intensive work with other alcoholics."

Throughout this book, we've worked hard to build a strong foundation; one that includes humility and accountability, a base of structure, and willingness to try new things. We've then taken it a step further by suggesting how to proactively deal with potential disappointments. Now, as we look back on what we have built for ourselves through this book and our other programs, we realize it was never intended to be kept a secret.

We are called to pass it along; beckoned to a life of

service to others.

As you begin to find new and exciting ways to pay forward the blessings you miraculously received, you will realize your foundation has become stronger and stronger. Like liquid concrete slowly hardening into a sidewalk, your footing will find stability and balance. Giving yourself away should be the cornerstone of your recovery. This gift freely given to you is not yours to keep, but to share.

Two of the greatest examples of "carrying the message" I've seen are Joe Pellow and Chris Flannery. Both of these outstanding men have devoted their lives to giving back to alcoholics and addicts. Both men own sober-living homes, and furthermore they both reside in the homes with the men. This ensures each resident has the maximum amount of mentoring and guidance possible.

I first met Joe while I was a client at Rob's Ranch. Weekly he would come out and visit the guys in treatment. Joe's a soft-spoken, gentle kind of guy, so when he talked, a genuine sense of compassion and understanding filled the room. Joe has devoted his life to helping people get back on their feet and reclaim their lives, living intentionally with the residents of his sober-living homes, patiently guiding them to get their feet underneath them financially, emotionally, and spiritually. Guys from all ages, backgrounds, and walks of life have passed through his program, and each one of them have been given specific attention and direction from Joe. His legacy of compassion and generosity has been passed along to countless families as he has helped lay a firm foundation for literally hundreds of men over the past ten years.

Just like my story, saying YES was a huge part of Joe's story as well. After committing to recovery, Joe discovered that he longed to be around other people in recovery, a longing that propelled him down his road to a life of service. Within a few months into his journey, a mentor asked him to consider opening a sober-living home. What do you think Joe said? YES, of course! He jumped at the chance. Ten years and innumerable changed lives later, Joe still passionately pursues men in need of a safe and structured environment to spend their early days of recovery. I am one of those men, so thank you Joe for all you have done. You are great man!

In the same vein, Chris opened a sober-living home.

Every week for several years, Chris has traveled to two treatment centers: Clay Crossing or Rob's Ranch and sometimes both, faithfully delivering his message of hope and life-change through Jesus Christ. He's a welcome sight to the men and staff of the facilities, because he never fails to bring tons of soda, chips, and goodies to brighten their day.

A few years into his recovery, Chris found that his love for serving others carried over to his home church, where he began serving a few times a month before taking it up a notch and serving at six different services throughout the weekend. I truly can't think of any one man who more embodies the spirit of servanthood than Chris Flannery.

As you can see, neither Joe nor Chris took the theory of "giving back" lightly. They both grabbed hold of their new lifestyles and made it their mission to minister to other addicts and alcoholics. They chose to do it by opening homes and fostering a safe and structured environment for men as they learned to live life again.

But this isn't the only way you can give back. There are thousands of possibilities and needs you can fill within the recovery community. As a newbie, one way I found to "give back" was through living my new life out in the open, stripping the label of anonymous and proudly proclaiming my restored identity. For many of you, the freshness of your new life will charge you to shout it from the mountaintops. Proclaiming for all to hear that you are sober, you have changed, and you are darn proud of it will inspire and give courage to those who desperately need it.

If you opt to keep it on the down-low, to re-emerge into society silently and subtly, that's your choice. It's completely up to you how you go about it. As I have tried to do throughout this book, I can only share what has worked for me.

Just as in other walks of life, in recovery you have a choice about promoting your recovery freedom. This may be a way for you not only to spread a positive message to others, but also to serve as another layer of accountability. That is the main reason I decided to live my recovery in the public eye. Yes, it is risky, and if relapse finds you, it could devastate a lot of people. You need to consider that.

But I knew I needed all the accountability I could possibly muster, so from the get-go, I told everyone who would listen who I used to be and who I am today. This not only gave me an incredible amount of accountability, but also quickly gave me a platform in which I could carry the message. The more I spread my story, the more opportunities came for me to give back.

It just felt right from the beginning. Everyday life

seemed so fresh and new. Opportunity seemed abundant. After *years* of living in the dark, the light was so warm and inviting that I couldn't get enough. I threw myself out there and said YES to anything and everything people asked me to do. I shared my story in countless places: I posted about my life in recovery through social media and started a blog where I opened my life up and tried to speak honestly about my past and how I was overcoming the various trials I encountered.

The magic behind giving back is how it strengthens you. So whether your personality is similar to mine or not, I challenge you to push yourself beyond what you are accustomed. Stretch yourself and see what happens. Maybe, like me, by letting the whole world know your story and living a life of transparency, you will find an elevated level of accountability. You may feel tension when everyone knows about your past, but maybe that will help you stay grounded and draw a hedge of protection around you.

Maybe you have a gift for writing. Start a blog and share your story of recovery. People who need it will find it. Talk about where you have come from and what's helped you overcome. Who knows how many people you could touch?

One thing is for sure. Each of us has a tribe, a

following. This might include your family, friends, social networks, co-workers, church buddies, etc. Within everyone's tribe there is a person who is either struggling with addiction themselves or who knows someone close to them that is struggling.

Trust me on this one. As I began to post about my recovery and send out inspirational notes about my progress, countless people reached out to me. Many were congratulatory and gave me great motivation; but the majority reached out privately and expressed how they needed help or told me that a loved one was in trouble.

I've been so blessed to work with dozens of old high school buddies and folks from my hometown. Every now and then I help them find treatment or set a course of action for their brother or their uncle to follow, but most of the time, I just lend a compassionate ear. I can't tell you the joy I feel when those phones calls and visits end. It's boundless. The satisfaction and boost in confidence are off the charts, and it's all because I gave myself away.

I understand not every profession or personal circumstance will allow you to publicly proclaim your newfound sobriety. I get that, and as I mentioned in the introduction, you have to use your own discretion when applying these principles. However, I believe there is something to be said about living your new life out in the open, freely giving to everyone you come in contact with.

Addict or not, we've all been given an amazing gift—a brand-new existence—and with that comes responsibility and with that responsibility comes influence. Courageously sharing our stories of hope and passing along lessons we've learned should become an innate part of our existence.

If you look closely you will see this benevolent spirit present in a variety of areas today. Take these two organizations for example...

The first is the organization called TED. This group started out in 1984 in an effort to bring together individuals from the three worlds of **Technology, Entertainment** and **Design** to present new ideas. By 1990, a yearly conference was established and soon it was open to any individual who could deliver an impactful and enlightened presentation within eighteen minutes. New ideas, inventions, and strategies were unveiled, and soon this yearly ideafest became one of the most exclusive tickets to find. The event became such a huge success they decided to start sharing these powerful presentations online. As of 2011, the now-famous and ubiquitous TED Talks have raked in over 50 million views online.

So what happened? What pushed them over the edge? What gave them the fuel they needed to propel themselves from an average once-in-a-while event to the most exclusive conference in the world, producing millions of views every day on their website? It was the principle of "radical openness."

This principle pushed them to not only give away their product (videos of individual presentations) but to hand out their brand, methods, and formats.

For TED, "radical openness" has been a process. The initial courageous step of posting its speakers' talks online caused massive amounts of stress for management and many worried that people would not continue to pay to come to the conferences. Why pay for something you can get free? What ended up happening, however, was totally the opposite. As they began to give away what had made them so successful, the demand began to increase exponentially.

The next step in the process propelled TED to an even higher level of influence and enabled them to educate and enlighten thousands of more people. They began to "give away their brand" with a new venture called TEDx, which allowed anyone to apply for a license to hold their own TED conference. The European director of TED Talks, Bruno Giussani, said this about what happened when they started practicing radical openness: "We found that by giving stuff away, we received even more in return. We have a huge committed community, a lot of brand recognition, and the capacity to touch communities where we had no contact before… We've gone from two conferences to 4500 TEDxs. The more you open your processes up, the more you co-opt other people, the more you receive in return."

What a great story of giving back. The folks at TED could have very easily slapped an iTunes-esque 99-cent charge onto every video they had acquired throughout the years. They had the rights; it was their idea to produce this ingenious idea summit. Tons of revenue could have theoretically poured in the doors, but instead they chose to give away what they had received and created. They opened the flow of ideas to tribes all across the country who never would have never been able to make it to California for the main event. This principle of radical openness has boosted this organization to a stratosphere of influence never before seen in the conference industry.

Another example of the power of giving back can be

found in the success of a church called LifeChurch.tv. Taking their cue from the biblical principle of tithing that states an individual or a family should give back 10% of its earnings to a local church, LifeChurch.tv adopted a model of openness when it came to their resources in 2008.

Prior to this time the church, which had started with fewer than 30 people meeting in a glorified two-car garage in 1995, had exploded to over 10,000 weekly attendees meeting in multiple locations throughout the US. Due to this unbelievable level of growth, the church was naturally forced to expand resources and teams and begin to produce tons of curricula. They needed to create new and different ways in which to keep up with the dramatic flow of congregants.

They did so marvelously and soon were not only one of the fastest-growing churches in America, but were also setting the pace when it came to innovation in the church world. They initiated the multi-location movement, opened a church location online, and began using video and creative content for each sermon series.

As their popularity grew, LifeChurch.tv decided to take a dramatic shift against the norm and stopped packaging their content for sale. Instead they started giving it away for free.

This cultural shift was also an innovative move that propelled them to even greater heights. Since that decision was made, attendance has doubled and a plethora of new locations have sprung up, making LifeChurch.tv now one of the largest churches in the world.

At the time of this writing, over 10,000 churches now use LifeChurch.tv's resources in one way or another. They are reaching more and more people by allowing smaller churches to use their sermons, worship music, children's curriculum, graphics, and more. In a similar fashion to the folks at TED, LifeChurch.tv took it up a notch and began to give the Bible away, using their own financial resources to create and market a free Bible app for smartphones and tablets called YouVersion. As I write this, this app has been downloaded to over 75 million devices! Talk about giving back without expecting anything in return. Wow!

TED and LifeChurch.tv are two organizations that really seem to understand what life is all about. They realized that the blessings of success go hand in hand with the responsibility of influence. We must follow these examples and pass along freely our resources, time, and energy to all those in need, generously giving back to those who could put into practice our new ideas and creations.

The Big Book again sums it up well when speaking to this charge to give it away: "Never avoid these responsibilities, but be sure you are doing the right thing if you assume them. Helping others is the foundation stone of your recovery. A kindly act once in a while isn't enough. You have to act the Good Samaritan every day, if need be."

This way of life is really why I started writing this book in the first place. As I looked back on my first couple years in sobriety, I realized I had overcome quite a bit. I'd experienced some difficult times and was blessed to accomplish some incredible achievements. Within each story was a lesson learned that was not meant to be kept to myself. No, it was given to me so I could pass it along to you.

Your story is no different. You've walked this earth and experienced a life no other man or woman in the world has ever experienced. Your story is unique. Your gifts are distinct. You, my friend, are special… and someone needs *you*. Just as I hope my story and suggestions have helped you stay strong and helped you build a firm foundation, your story and suggestions can do the same for hundreds of others out there struggling to find their way.

Don't keep it to yourself. Give it away!

CHALLENGE

They say it's better to give than to receive so that is what we are going to practice today.

1) Set aside some time later today or tomorrow and begin to write your story. It doesn't have to be a long, perfectly crafted novel. Just be yourself. Below are some tips to help you get started:

- Who did you use to be?
- Where did you come from?
- Who raised you?
- What hobbies/activities/ were you into?
- What was your character like?
- What happened?
- When did you start using?
- Did something happen to hurt you?
- How did your using progress?
- What were the ramifications?
- Who are you now?
- Did you find help?
- Who gave it to you? (rehab, intervention,

etc.)

- What did you learn?

- What are you doing today?

2) Be bold. Once your story is done, share it with someone. Here's a list of safe places where you can share your experiences, your strength, and your hope. Remember, what you have, someone else needs. Don't be selfish; give it away...

- AA/NA meetings

- Celebrate Recovery meetings

- Church

- Small groups

- A local treatment center

- A detox facility

3) When you've finished your story, if you feel compelled, email it to me (my address is in the back of this book) and, with your permission, I will post it on our website: HopeIsAlive. net. We'd love to read about what you have gone through and hear what's helped you stay strong throughout your recovery. This huge step will empower you to reclaim your past,

and then allow you to begin to use it to help other people. As others begin to read your story, they will relate to your trials and find hope that better days are ahead. As we saw with the organizations detailed in this chapter, by taking the courageous step to submit your story, you will be impacting the lives of people all across the world.

GIVE IT AWAY!!!

Spiritual Application

"This is how much God loved the world: He gave his Son, his one and only Son. And this is why: so to that no one need be destroyed; by believing in him, anyone can have a whole and lasting life. God didn't go to all the trouble of sending his Son merely to point an accusing finger, telling the world how bad it was. He came to help, to put the world right again. Anyone who trusts in him is acquitted..." –John 3:16-18a (MSG)

Give it away. I love the sound of that phrase. We have so much to give away. I realize many of you feel you have been shafted in life, and certainly life has a way of dumping on us. However, we also have a great deal of blessings given to us. As addicts we are often very self-centered; giving away takes the focus off *us* and puts it on *others*.

Whether it is a listening ear or a sounding board, *you* have a lot to give. Please don't strictly connect giving with monetary things. Sometimes the greatest gifts cost no money. Have you considered giving someone the benefit of the doubt? What about giving a second chance? The most fun way to give is anonymously. I'm a big fan of random acts of kindness.

As we "give it away" we are passing on the love others have given us. Indeed, the greatest example of "giving it away" the world has ever known is the gift of life given to all of creation from the Father of Lights. As the familiar verse above details, God gave the world His son. Jesus.

God knew we desperately needed hope and redemption, so he gave it—freely—for *all of us* to receive.

Everyone.

That means you.

If you haven't accepted it, I urge you to do so today.

Claim this gift of life God gave us.

Gave you.

He gave it away.

Will you take it?

CHAPTER 9

HOPE IS ALIVE!

Let me close by asking you some questions.

Are you ready to escape fear and find rest in freedom?

Are you sick of being scared?

Do you really think at your age you will have another chance?

Do you want to die or live?

Do you think your kids deserve this?

Is she worth what this is doing to you?

Do you really want to stay sober?

Honestly, do you really want this?

I hope your answer to the last question is a resounding YES! If that's the case then I will end this book with one last challenge. Here it is.

How are you going to keep hope alive in your life?

My hope sprang to back to life when I got sober in

April of 2011. The darkness that had engulfed me for years vanished. With each passing day, the promise of Jeremiah 29:11 became more and more of a reality. As I grew confident, my addiction grew weaker and weaker, and I began to see that, like that scripture promises, I *did* have a future. I have a purpose. My life *matters*.

I began to understand that I could actually do something I was proud of for once.

Early on, I was barely able to wipe the smile off my face as I bowed to pray every night. The joy just overflowed from my body. I was bursting with happiness. I couldn't believe I had so many friends who actually cared about me. I could not believe people would actually trust me again. They shouldn't have, but they did anyway and that felt good! It was all just so crazy.

I will never forget the feeling I had when I hit six months of sobriety. It was magical! I stared down at my phone, reading over and over the words "six months," and my eyes got blurry and tears streamed down my face. I looked up at my mom who standing there with me and I told her, "I never in my wildest imagination thought I would ever see this day."

What a miracle!

Life just kept getting better month by month. More peace, more hope, more love poured in. It was as if I was an empty pitcher and God was pouring in gallon after gallon of water. I was refreshed, restored, and ready to take on the world. And in a lot of ways, I did.

In my early sobriety, I went after things that would have left me in the fetal position during my addiction. Asking for meetings with bold leaders, taking on an impossible job, speaking in front of hundreds of people... writing a book! But with each step, God's presence became stronger. He never left me and always proved himself faithful. Even when I was hurt and humiliated, God stayed with me. Even when I yelled and screamed at Him, *Why?! Why?! Why?!* He patiently listened and responded with love. He never left me, never. Not once.

And that's really the essence of my story. How my hope is alive today.

No matter how hard I tried to pull my hand away from God's grasp, He never let go.

Although my body was facing the other direction and covered in sin, He never let go.

When I took off running countless times to seek shelter from the reality I had perpetuated, He never let go.

When I blatantly went against His will over and over and over again, He never let go.

So I know today: my hope can rest in the fact that *God is for me.* He loves me no matter what I have done. He will never leave me and that keeps my hope alive.

The same holds true for you. God loves you. He's never left, nor will He ever, no matter what your past looks like or how much baggage you have in your closet.

He's seen everything we've ever done and still loves us just the same.

As I close, I want you to know I believe in each of these principles we've discussed throughout this book. They've held me together so many times when I was weak. I have leaned on what I've learned from countless people over the past few years and have combined standards of proven programs and theories. As a result I have found a practical way to stay sober.

That's what you have to do as well. I've said it consistently throughout this book: there are dozens of quality programs out there that will assist you in recovery. Your task is to find the right one or combination that works best for you.

The courage to say YES worked for me time and

time again. The visual signs of encouragement I made and the mandate I repeated thousands of times have carried me along one day at a time. My dream team has kept me in line, encouraging and supporting me through disappointing days. Admitting my story thrust me into a place of service whereby each hand I held or hug I gave emboldened me to press on.

In the end these tools saved, and continue to save, my life; but they didn't save my soul. Only a personal relationship with Jesus will do that. Get to know Him, I promise the more you do the more you'll like him.

You're Worth It

As you walk down the road to recovery, you must walk with your eyes wide open and your head held high, always focused on what lies ahead, not what you've left behind. Keeping hope alive in your life will take work. It's not always an easy road and it's certainly the road less traveled.

But it can be done.

Take comfort in the fact that *many* before you have found success and have done so in a variety of different ways. Just as God has made you specifically unique, He has also created a diverse collection of tools for addicts like you and me to maintain our sobriety.

Your recovery is in your hands. It's *your* choice how successful you will be. Many around you will fail; it's sad but the reality of the situation. However, *that doesn't have to be the case for you.* You can be the one.

You can make it. I believe in you!

I hope I've helped you build a strong foundation from which to move forward. Maybe a few tools you can use along the way. When it comes down to your recovery it is just that... it is yours. It's on you. You have the power. You hold the keys to the kingdom.

But you know what?

You're worth fighting for! God made you so spectacularly special, your mind can't even fathom it. His plans for you are going blow your mind as you begin to see them come together. Those prosperous plans of renewing relationships, completing your education, fulfilling careers, finding your soul mate and the rest of your wildest dreams are all within your reach. Your life can be full of hope, full of victories, full of freedom.

You're worth all of that. I would even say you deserve it.

Yeah, that's right: *you*.

One Last Time

Here is a recap of what helped me. I hope these tools and the stories I've shared from my life have helped revive the hope inside of you. It's my prayer and desire that you go forward from this moment on, living the life you've always desired.

As you do, keep these tools handy. I promise you never know when you might need them.

- *Surrender daily.* Give up the fight; your old ways don't work.
- *Hope Partners.* Build a strong team of supporters around you. It takes a village to raise a child.
- *Get a routine.* Prayer, reflection, correction. Repeat.
- *Make a mandate.* "I will not use no matter what."
- *Just say YES.* Put yourself out there; you never know what lies on the other side of a YES!
- *Keep the peace.* Proactively take steps to squash

future disappointments.

- *Give it away.* The gifts of sobriety are not yours to keep; they must be shared.

May the road rise to meet you
May the wind be always at your back,
May the sun shine warm upon your face
May the rains fall soft upon your fields
And until we meet again
May God hold you in the palm of His hand.

Lance Lang,

A broken and forgiven man

Spiritual Application

Yep, hope is alive and I testify to that fact. Hope is a strange thing. The result of hope has everything to do with the object in which we place our hope. If you place your faith or hope in something lame, then don't expect to have stellar results.

But a hope and faith placed in something eternal will yield eternal fruit. By now you have figured out that my hope

162

is in Jesus Christ. Sure lots of people define God in their own way. For me hope and faith go together.

Through all of or miscues, mistakes and mess-ups there is always the clear, present, and consistent hope that with God *all* things are possible.

APPENDIX

RECOMMENDED TREATMENT CENTERS

Want to get sober but don't know who to call? I fully
endorse *any* of the treatment centers below:

Rob's Ranch

405-253-3838

www.RobsRanch.org

Valley Hope Association

800-544-5101

www.ValleyHope.org

Clay Crossing

866-374-1220

www.ClayCrossing.com

Santé Center for Healing

800-258-4250

www.SanteCenter.com

ACKNOWLEDGMENTS

Mom and Dad: Thank you for allowing your 30-year-old son to move back in with you, for dealing with me throughout this process, and for carefully listening to every crazy idea that came into my head. Your support and encouragement mean everything to me. I love you both so much! I've never seen parents like you guys. You both are the absolute best! Thank you for being the perfect example in every walk of life.

Ally: What can I say… you are the only one who has seen it all. No one knows me like you do. The fact that you are still willing to be seen in public with me is evidence enough of the beautiful, forgiving person you are. I love you, best friend!

Leah and Nick: Time after time I have disappointed you both, but you've never given up on me. Leah, you inspire me every time I see you, and Nick, well, you're the brother I always wanted. In fact, you're better. I love you both!

Pat: I am dead without you, my friend. That's just the

way it is. Thank you for being bold enough to follow your heart and ask the tough questions. You are a mighty leader! Love you, man!

Adam Palmer: Thank you for making this dream a reality and sharing your wonderful gift with me. I hope this is the first of many journeys we travel.

Scott Williams: Thank you for telling me I had story to tell and helping me tell it. Let's keep this thing going...

Jim Riley: Thank you for dealing with this punk the past two years. For all the time and energy you have invested in me and the thousands of others the past thirty years. Your legacy will live on through all of us forever.

Dick Liddell: Thank you for changing my life. Both stays at Rob's Ranch completely altered the course of my life, in the best possible ways. I don't know where I would be if it wasn't for that place. Thank you for always believing in me, and for your endless encouragement. Your words have always held a special place in my heart.

Israel Hogue: I love you, bro! You helped me find my heart again. Thank you so much! The best is yet to be...

My boys: This book is as much your story as it is mine. We've walked this journey together. Thank you all for inspiring me, correcting me, loving me and encouraging me. I love each one of you and will always have your back. I wish I could list every single one of you… but you know who you are. One day at a time boys, one day at a time…

BIOGRAPHY

A recovering addict himself, Lance Lang is currently the Executive Director of "Hope is Alive", a non-profit organization devoted to supporting men and women recovering from all types of addictions. He is also a sought- after speaker, marketing consultant for several businesses, non-profits, and churches, and is the Recovery Pastor at Sanctuary Church in Oklahoma City, Oklahoma. His website LanceLang.com is read by thousands each week.

LANCE LANG

WWW.LANCELANG.COM
LANCE@LANCELANG.COM
@LANCELANG

Made in the USA
Charleston, SC
12 April 2013